Peggy Dymond Leavey

Born in Toronto, Peggy Dymond Leavey was one of five children in a family where books and reading were an important part of everyday life. While still a youngster, she discovered a love of writing.

Her first book, *The Movie Years,* grew out of her love of history, and she has been a contributing editor for three books of local history. Her numerous articles and short stories have been published in newspapers, magazines, and anthologies. Peggy is also the author of nine novels for young readers, including *Sky Lake Summer, The Deep End Gang,* and *The Path Through the Trees,* all of which were nominated for the Silver Birch Award. *Growing Up Ivy,* published by Dundurn in 2010, was a starred selection in the Canadian Children's Book Centre's *Best Books for Kids & Teens, 2011.*

Peggy has two previous Quest Biographies to her credit: *Mary Pickford: Canada's Silent Siren, America's Sweetheart* and *Laura Secord: Heroine of the War of 1812,* which was shortlisted for the 2013 Speaker's Book Award.

For seventeen years Peggy worked as a librarian in Prince Edward County. She continues to be a member of The Writers' Union of Canada, the Canadian Society of Children's Authors, Illustrators & Performers (CANSCAIP), the Spirit of the Hills Writers' Group, and a number of local arts associations.

Peggy and her husband live near Trenton, Ontario, where she enjoys reading, writing, the outdoors (in go time with her family.

In the same collection

Ray Argyle, *Joey Smallwood: Schemer and Dreamer*
Ven Begamudré, *Isaac Brock: Larger Than Life*
Kate Braid, *Emily Carr: Rebel Artist*
Edward Butts, *Henry Hudson: New World Voyager*
Edward Butts, *Simon Girty: Wilderness Warrior*
Anne Cimon, *Susanna Moodie: Pioneer Author*
Deborah Cowley, *Lucille Teasdale: Doctor of Courage*
Gary Evans, *John Grierson: Trailblazer of Documentary Film*
Julie H. Ferguson, *James Douglas: Father of British Columbia*
Judith Fitzgerald, *Marshall McLuhan: Wise Guy*
lian goodall, *William Lyon Mackenzie King: Dreams and Shadows*
Tom Henighan, *Vilhjalmur Stefansson: Arctic Adventurer*
Stephen Eaton Hume, *Frederick Banting: Hero, Healer, Artist*
Naïm Kattan, *A.M. Klein: Poet and Prophet*
Betty Keller, *Pauline Johnson: First Aboriginal Voice of Canada*
Heather Kirk, *Mazo de la Roche: Rich and Famous Writer*
Valerie Knowles, *William C. Van Horne: Railway Titan*
Vladimir Konieczny, *Glenn Gould: A Musical Force*
D.H. Lahey, *George Simpson: Blaze of Glory*
Wayne Larsen, *A.Y. Jackson: A Love for the Land*
Wayne Larsen, *James Wilson Morrice: Painter of Light and Shadow*
Wayne Larsen, *Tom Thomson: Artist of the North*
Peggy Dymond Leavey, *Laura Secord: Heroine of the War of 1812*
Peggy Dymond Leavey, *Mary Pickford: Canada's Silent Siren, America's Sweetheart*
Francine Legaré, *Samuel de Champlain: Father of New France*
Margaret Macpherson, *Nellie McClung: Voice for the Voiceless*
Nicholas Maes, *Robertson Davies: Magician of Words*
Dave Margoshes, *Tommy Douglas: Building the New Society*
Marguerite Paulin, *René Lévesque: Charismatic Leader*
Raymond Plante, *Jacques Plante: Behind the Mask*
Jim Poling Sr., *Tecumseh: Shooting Star, Crouching Panther*
Tom Shardlow, *David Thompson: A Trail by Stars*
Arthur Slade, *John Diefenbaker: An Appointment with Destiny*
Roderick Stewart, *Wilfrid Laurier: A Pledge for Canada*
Sharon Stewart, *Louis Riel: Firebrand*
Nathan Tidridge, *Prince Edward, Duke of Kent: Father of the Canadian Crown*
André Vanasse, *Gabrielle Roy: A Passion for Writing*
John Wilson, *John Franklin: Traveller on Undiscovered Seas*
John Wilson, *Norman Bethune: A Life of Passionate Conviction*

A QUEST BIOGRAPHY

MOLLY BRANT

MOHAWK LOYALIST AND DIPLOMAT

PEGGY DYMOND LEAVEY

DUNDURN
TORONTO

Unless otherwise credited, photos are by the author.

Project Editor: Allison Hirst
Copy Editor: Jess Shulman
Design: Laura Boyle
Printer: Webcom
Cover Design: Carmen Giraudy

Library and Archives Canada Cataloguing in Publication

Leavey, Peggy Dymond, author
          Molly Brant : Mohawk loyalist and diplomat / Peggy Dymond Leavey.

(A quest biography)
Includes bibliographical references and index. Issued in print and electronic formats.
ISBN 978-1-4597-2893-6 (pbk.).--ISBN 978-1-4597-2894-3 (pdf).--
ISBN 978-1-4597-2895-0 (epub)

1. Brant, Molly, 1736-1796. 2. Mohawk women--Biography. 3. United Empire loyalists--Biography. I. Title. II. Series: Quest biography .

E99.M8L42 2015   971.004'9755420092   C2015-900573-6
                                                                                      C2015-900574-4

1   2   3   4   5   19   18   17   16   15

Conseil des Arts du Canada   Canada Council for the Arts

ONTARIO ARTS COUNCIL
CONSEIL DES ARTS DE L'ONTARIO
an Ontario government agency
un organisme du gouvernement de l'Ontario

We acknowledge the support of the Canada Council for the Arts and the Ontario Arts Council for our publishing program. We also acknowledge the financial support of the Government of Canada through the Canada Book Fund and Livres Canada Books, and the Government of Ontario through the Ontario Book Publishing Tax Credit and the Ontario Media Development Corporation.

Printed and bound in Canada.

VISIT US AT
Dundurn.com | Definingcanada.ca | @dundurnpress | Facebook.com/dundurnpress

Dundurn
3 Church Street, Suite 500
Toronto, Ontario, Canada
M5E 1M2

To Carter James Jeffrey Cloutier,
the first of the new generation.
And for Wayne, always.

She seldom imposed herself into the picture,
but no one was in her presence
without being aware of her.
(description of Molly Brant, circa 1763)

Contents

Acknowledgements

Early in the writing of this book I was intrigued to discover the research done by another Molly Brant enthusiast. Celia B. File made Molly the subject of her master's thesis for Queen's University in 1930. A white woman, File had lived for seven years among the Mohawks on the Bay of Quinte in the 1920s and taught school there. "The thesis was accepted," she wrote, "but I cannot say it was completed, for the woman will not let me alone."

Later, a Mohawk elder remembered that the teacher had been writing a book about Molly Brant. Unfortunately, the manuscript of the book was destroyed in a house fire when Celia File lived in Oil Springs, Ontario. She never felt well enough to rewrite it.

I want to thank Joyce Waddell-Townsend of Kingston for sharing her knowledge of the history of that city and for knowing all the best people to contact. Among the historic homes and buildings Joyce showed me during my visit was the Anglican Cathedral of St. George, where she is a tour guide.

My thanks, as well, go to Susan M. Bazely, member of the Association of Professional Archaeologists, for answering my questions, for sharing her own research on Molly Brant, and for pointing out on a map of Kingston all the places I should see.

Thank you to my editors, Jess Shulman and Dundurn's Allison Hirst, for their kind and careful editing. Allison, you always make my writing better. Thank you to Lisa Russell of the Anglican Diocese of Ontario Archives for her assistance, and to the staff at the Queen's University Archives, the Kanhiote Tyendinaga Territory Public Library, and the Lennox and Addington County Museum and Archives.

I am grateful to photographer Mark Bergin for generously providing the photograph that graces the cover of this book. A special thanks to Jeff W. Leavey, my son, for the hand-drawn map of "Key Locations in Molly Brant's World" that appears in the book, to my sister Mary McColl for giving me a place to stay and for going along on my self-guided walking tour of Kingston, and to my husband, Wayne Leavey, for the trips to the Mohawk Valley and the tour of the British forts in the Champlain Valley where I was soaking up atmosphere.

And I want to acknowledge Alan Brant (Anataras) and Betty Maracle (Katsitsiase), facilitators of the course "Aboriginal Awareness" at Loyalist College where they shared their understanding of the Mohawk culture. *Niaweh*/thank you.

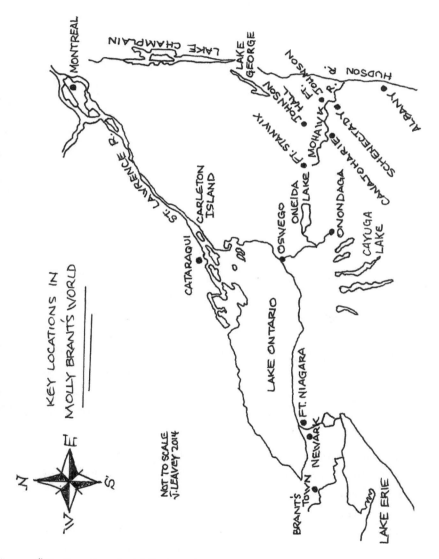

"*Key Locations in Molly Brant's World.*"

Prologue

It is a fine day in 1831. Two women step down from a carriage that has pulled up in front of a manor house in the Mohawk Valley of central New York State.

Margaret Farley and her travelling companion are both in their mid-sixties, Margaret the widow of Captain George Farley of the 60th (Royal American) Regiment of Foot. She is also the third daughter of Molly Brant, Mohawk Loyalist and diplomat, the woman who is credited with keeping her Native people on the side of the British during the American Revolution, and Sir William Johnson, one of the most influential men in British North America in the eighteenth century.

The women hesitate on the shoulder of grass, looking up at the house. Flanked by two stone blockhouses, Johnson Hall is a frame structure, Georgian in style and painted grey, its wooden facade cut to look like stone.

This bust of Molly Brant is located in the east courtyard of the Rideaucrest Home in Kingston. It faces the Cataraqui River, as did Molly's home.

Her companion hears Margaret's sharp intake of breath. "Are you all right, my dear?"

"Oh, yes. Quite fine. It's just ... well ... it's so much *smaller* than I remember." Margaret gives a rueful smile. "I was just seven when we fled the Valley. I've kept this place in my mind all these years as the grandest house in all the land, bigger than any house in Montreal. I've never forgotten it. And now I blush to think of all the lies I've told about it."

In a few days Margaret Farley will leave for England to be with her children. She knows she will likely never return and has asked her friend to make the trip from Montreal with her in order to see the family home one last time.

Ten years later, in 1841, when she is settled in England, Margaret will tell the story of the flight she and her family made from the Mohawk Valley on the eve of the American Revolution.

"Shortly after my father's death in 1774," she begins, "we left Johnson Hall, and Mother took us all back to her former home in Canajoharie. Mother insisted on staying on her own property there in the little Mohawk village, even though she'd been warned by General Herkimer, a neighbour and former friend, that her life was in danger. Mother was not afraid, though, and she promised Herkimer that she would remain neutral, the wish of most of the Six Nations people. She would not side with either the British or the Colonials.

"This wasn't enough for Herkimer, however, and he threatened her repeatedly that if we didn't leave, we'd all be taken to the jail in Albany. Can you imagine?

"One night, shortly after we'd all gone to bed, someone came banging on our door, and several men entered the house, demanding of Mother to know the whereabouts of her brother, Captain Joseph Brant. He was not with us, and Mother invited the men to search the house if they didn't believe her. They did just that, beginning their search in the sleeping rooms, drawing back the curtains on our beds. Of course all they found was us children. I was terrified.

"A few nights later Mother got word that we were to be forcibly removed on a specific night, even told the exact hour they would come for us. Immediately, she sent us to the safety of the home of a trusted friend. She and the servants remained behind, keeping watch through the night.

"When Mother sent the servants to see how we were doing they told us that at two o'clock in the morning they'd seen several persons outside Mother's house. No one had entered, but we were so frightened by the servants' tale that we all scrambled back into our clothes, convinced that we were about to be seized by these unknown persons. The neighbour hid us behind a screen in a nook in her house until Mother could send for us the next day.

"Mother knew it was no longer safe for us to stay in the country. We fled Canajoharie — Mother, seven children, and our four servants. As we began our journey, we passed within sight of Johnson Hall. It broke our hearts to see lights in the windows of our former home. Someone else was living there, and we — the rightful owners — were sneaking away in the dark, in fear for our lives."

1

Mohawk Childhood

Details of where Molly Brant was born and who her father was remain sketchy, at best. The year of her birth most generally accepted is 1736. Authorities agree that her mother's name was Margaret (Sahetagearat Onagsakearat or Owandah) and that both her parents were Christian Mohawks living in the Upper Castle, the village of Canajoharie, one of the two main Mohawk villages in central New York State.

The Lower Castle, Tionderoga, was located thirty miles downstream, at the place where Schoharie Creek meets the Mohawk River. After a fort was built there in 1710, the old town was more commonly known as Fort Hunter.

(In earlier times, a number of Native towns had been protected by stockades, surrounded by ramparts, and so heavily fortified that the English used to refer to them as "castles." That term continued in use into the eighteenth century.)

Records from Queen Anne's Chapel at Fort Hunter show the

baptism of "Mary," the daughter of Margaret and "Cannassware," on April 13, 1775. Although some biographers have suggested that this is our Molly, that is unlikely, considering Molly Brant herself gave her age as forty-seven on the "Return of Loyalists on Carleton Island," recorded in 1783.

Some sources suggest that Molly was not born in Canajoharie at all, but on the banks of the Ohio River, where later her brother Joseph was born.

At Molly's birth her parents gave her the Mohawk name Gonwatsijayenni, meaning "someone lends her a flower." In English she was known as Mary or, more often, Molly.

At birth a Mohawk child was given a baby name, one that was not already in use by the clan to which it belonged. Later, the child might take an adult name that was available, and the baby name would be returned to the clan to be used again. This might explain why sources refer to Molly Brant as both Gonwatsijayenni and Dagonwadonti, meaning "she against whom rival forces contend."

In March 1743, while seven-year-old Molly and her family were away from home on what may have been an extended hunting expedition to the Ohio Valley, Margaret gave birth to a son. She and her husband, Peter (Tehowaghwengaraghkwin), named the child Thayendanegea, which means "two sticks" or "he who places two bets" in Mohawk. He later became better known by his Christian name, Joseph.

Peter may well have been Molly's father, too, although there is no evidence to prove this. Margaret was most certainly the children's mother, and since in the matrilineal society of the Iroquois it is the mother's lineage that is important — the line through which one's descendants are traced — Joseph and Molly were brother and sister.

Within the Iroquois Confederacy, each member nation — Seneca, Cayuga, Onondaga, Oneida, Mohawk, and Tuscarora (adopted in 1722) — had its own grouping of matrilineages, called clans. The original Five Nations had a total of nine clans, with the Mohawk and the Oneida having the same three — the Wolf, the Bear, and the Turtle. As was the custom, Molly and Joseph became part of their mother's Wolf Clan.

Each clan was headed by a senior woman, referred to in English as a clan mother or matron. She wasn't necessarily the oldest woman in the clan, but she was the one with the best skills in leadership and diplomacy. Among the privileges of the clan mother was the power to choose a new chief from the important lineages when the former chief died. She also had the power, after conferring with the other women in the clan, to depose him if he didn't prove satisfactory. Clan mothers had the authority to forbid male relatives from going to war and to stop a war if they felt it had gone on long enough. They were also the ones who decided how any captives were to be treated.

*

Canajoharie, the name of the town where Molly grew up, means "the pot that washes itself," and it refers to a large circular crater worn into the limestone riverbed by the force of the water that falls forty-five feet into Canajoharie Creek.

By the mid-eighteenth century, many Mohawk had begun to move north to towns along the St. Lawrence such as Kahnawake, across the river from Montreal. Canajoharie had a population of only 250 to 300 individuals living in single-family cabins along the south shore of the Mohawk River. Before too many more years had passed, the cabins would be replaced by comfortable frame houses with barns for the livestock and for storing the summer's harvest. The Mohawk no longer lived in their traditional longhouses, although these large structures, with their arched roofs and elm-bark coverings, were still used for ceremonies.

By 1750 most Canajoharie people had been baptized in the Anglican Church. Margaret and her husband Peter were listed in the Register of Anglican Mohawks as "Protestant Christians." Church records at Queen Anne's Chapel list other children born to the couple between the years of Molly's and Joseph's births. These children, baptized Jacob and Christina, are assumed to have died in infancy.

Sometime in the 1740s, Peter (Tehowaghwengaraghkwin) died, possibly during one of the widespread cholera or influenza epidemics that claimed the lives of many Native people who were in contact with the Europeans. Along with their guns, ammunition, and rum, the Europeans brought with them new diseases for which the indigenous people had no immunity.

Widowed, Margaret returned with Molly and Joseph to Canajoharie, where they could expect to find shelter among the members of her clan, according to Iroquois custom.

There is an old story that Margaret's grandfather was a Mohawk chief (sometimes referred to in English as a "sachem" or wise man). Sachems were not warriors, but rather peace chiefs. This man's name was King Hendrick (Theyanoguen), also known as Hendrick Peters. Theyanoguen is believed to have been born between 1680 and 1690. A member of the Bear Clan, he lived in Canajoharie and became an important mediator between the Mohawk and the English and an important ally of the British against the French. He died at the Battle of Lake George in 1755.

There is no record to support any relationship between Margaret and Theyanoguen, and some biographers claim that the parents of Molly and Joseph were "nobodies," undistinguished, making them unlikely offspring of anyone of high rank in the Iroquois Confederacy. In fact, the esteemed Joseph Brant, Molly's younger brother, was never a league chief or sachem. If on occasion he was referred to as Chief Joseph Brant, it was as a courtesy only.

In 1710, four Native sachems, three Mohawks and one Mohican, travelled to London with Colonel Peter Schuyler, a Dutchman and the mayor of Albany, to Queen Anne's court at St. James's Palace. It was the most important visit ever made to a European capital by any Native American nation.

The four Native leaders, dubbed "kings" by their hosts, spoke through Colonel Schuyler, their interpreter and friend, describing themselves as allies of the queen and ambassadors of their people.

A full account of their visit was written in 1710 (*The Four Kings of Canada*), and includes the address they made to the queen. Their reason for making the long and hazardous journey across the ocean (they reportedly lost a member of their delegation at sea) was to ask Queen Anne to help them drive the French out of their country.

Earlier, they said, they had rejoiced at hearing the queen was planning to send an army to "reduce" Canada (Quebec). In preparation, on their side of "the lake," they'd built forts, store houses, canoes, and bateaux. They'd waited a long time for the fleet from England that was to go against Quebec by sea while they themselves went by land, but at last they were told that Queen Anne had been prevented by "some important affair" from carrying out the plan that season. Now, they told the court, they feared the French would think them unable to make war against them.

The visitors presented Her Majesty with belts of wampum and suggested that if she ignored their request they and their families would be forced to either leave their country or stand neutral. Either choice, they said, would be against their inclinations.

The four "kings" warned also that their people were being wooed by French priests with presents and "insinuations" to come over to their religion. But they said if Queen Anne would send over some Church of England (Anglican) missionaries they would be made most welcome.

During their lengthy visit to London, where they took in all the sights, the four were treated as celebrities. Poems and songs were written about them, and the queen commissioned Dutch artist John Verelst, who was living in England, to paint individual portraits of the men. The oldest known surviving oil portraits of North American Natives, the paintings were purchased from England for Library and Archives Canada in 1977 by way of a special grant from the Canadian government.

As a result of the petitions of the four "kings," Fort Hunter was built on the site of the Mohawk village of Tionderoga, and a Chapel of the Mohawks established there. A year after their visit Queen Anne sent the Mohawk sachems a gift of a silver communion service for the chapel, engraved with the royal coat of arms and this inscription: "The Gift of Her Majesty Anne, by the Grace of God, of Great Britain, France and Ireland and of her Plantations in North America, Queen, to her Indian Chappel [*sic*] of the Mohawks."

Queen Anne, eager to promote the Protestant religion abroad, also sent gifts of bibles and prayer books, and passed the request for missionaries on to the Society for the Propagation of the Gospel in Foreign Parts (SPG).

*

After returning to Canajoharie, the widow Margaret discovered that food was scarce among her people, and she was forced to find a way to provide for herself and her two children. Native women were forbidden to hunt for game. The forest was considered the men's domain, although families might take part in the fall hunt together.

After both men and women had cleared the land, the fields in which they grew their crops were considered the domain of the women, as were the homes where they raised their children. The men were away much of the time, on the hunt or defending their villages.

Iroquois children, adored by both parents and well-treated (some might even say permissively), would be taken into the fields even as infants, strapped to wooden cradle boards on their mothers' backs. As soon as they were old enough the children would be given simple chores to do.

Margaret worked at whatever small jobs she could find, but the family was often faced with starvation. She may well have joined in the liquor trade and most certainly would have enlisted the children to help her dig for ginseng root. Ginseng could be exchanged for food and supplies at the trading posts and forts. There was a lucrative market in China for the medicinal root that grew wild in the Mohawk Valley.

Late in the 1740s Margaret married Lykus, or Lucas, a prominent war leader. Unfortunately, he was killed in May 1750 during a raid against the Mohawks' old enemy, the Catawba tribe, in the Carolinas. Some sources leave Molly's stepfather Lykus out of her story altogether, perhaps because the relationship was so short-lived.

On September 9, 1753, after already bearing his child (Jacob, baptized March 4, 1753), Margaret married Brant (Kanagaradunka), whose wife had recently died. Several years older than Margaret, Brant was a wealthy Mohawk sachem from the Turtle Clan, living in Tionderoga. He had a son, Nickus, from his earlier marriage.

Brant lived in a large two-storey house and dressed in the style of a white man. His clothing and the furniture in his home were said to be the equal of those of a middle-class European. There is some suggestion that he may have had some non-native ancestry, possibly Dutch. There is no further mention of Margaret and Brant's baby Jacob, and it is assumed that he died.

Molly was a teenager and Joseph about ten years old when Brant built Margaret and her children a big house in Canajoharie, the best house in town, with a stone foundation, glass in the windows, and interior walls of plaster.

A prosperous man with important connections to white traders and government officials, Brant was also a kind and considerate father. Whenever he returned from his business dealings with the white man, he brought presents home for his stepchildren. Life was now much easier for the family than it had been. No longer was it a constant struggle to find enough food to satisfy their bellies. Because of their relationship with Brant, Margaret and her children were raised to a higher level in the eyes of Iroquois society, and Molly and Joseph took as their surname the name of their stepfather.

By this time the village of Canajoharie was surrounded and greatly outnumbered by white Europeans, mostly German and Dutch farmers and traders. After their mother married Brant Kanagaradunka, Molly and Joseph were exposed to British and American influences more than ever. It didn't take long for them to feel equally comfortable among their Mohawk and white contemporaries and to move easily between the two cultures.

Living closer geographically to white settlements than did the other tribes of the Iroquois Confederacy, the Mohawk had already begun to adopt some European practices. They were raising domestic animals as a source of food, making some of their traditional clothing out of cloth that they bartered for at the trading posts, and they had exchanged their traditional bows and arrows for guns. There was no need now for clay pots when they could have kettles made of copper.

2

In the Beginning

Long ago, according to Iroquois legend, before the arrival of the white man here on Turtle Island, the Haudenosaunee, People of the Longhouse, lived on the western plains.

The Haudenosaunee, later called the Iroquois by the French, slowly began to migrate toward the east. Over the years as they travelled, the various tribes found places along the way to build their separate villages. The largest group settled near the mouth of the Oswego River, on the southern shore of Lake Ontario.

The land was bountiful, but eventually the game on which they depended grew scarce, and the different bands left to look for better hunting grounds. One band, the Mohawk, also called the People of the Flint, settled in what became known as Mohawk Valley, along the river that bears their name. Their northern boundary was Lake Ontario and the St. Lawrence River; the Hudson River formed their eastern boundary; and the Catskill

Mountains marked the border in the south. In the west, their boundary blended with that of the Oneida people.

The Onondaga and the Cayuga built their towns still farther to the west, with the Seneca settling along Canandaigua Lake. What today is central New York State became the home of the five Iroquois Nations. Over time these blood relatives became enemies, and there were many wars between them.

A breakaway group of Mohawk, tired of the endless fighting and killing, left Mohawk Valley and settled on the north shore of the Bay of Quinte, in what is today Tyendinaga Mohawk Territory. The area at the time was the home of the Hurons, the Wyandot people. Here, sometime in the mid-fifteenth century, on December 21, the most powerful day of the year, the Peacemaker was born. A messenger from the Creator told his grandmother that this baby was special, that he had an important job to do. His grandmother named him "Deganahwideh."

When the boy was old enough he would help his mother grow their sacred tobacco. He was kind and honest and had great knowledge. He spent much time alone, receiving from the Creator the parts of his message, learning how he would tell the people how to live in peace and harmony, and asking for clarity about his mission. He shared what he knew with the older people, until one day he realized that his teaching days were over.

The story goes that he spent a year building a canoe, carving it out of white stone. The fact that the canoe floated proved the truth of his mission.

At sunrise one morning the boy left his village and paddled his stone canoe across the Beautiful Lake (Lake Ontario) and up the Oswego River, crossing Oneida Lake and portaging to the Mohawk River. Arriving in the land of the Mohawk, he told the people he had come to establish The Great Peace among the Iroquois. His message had three parts: peace, power, and righteousness.

A second man, named Hiawatha, or Ayonwatha — a Mohawk living in Onondaga — heard that the Peacemaker was coming and he went to Mohawk Valley to meet him. The Peacemaker taught his message to Ayonwatha, and together the two men gave the people the laws that formed The Great Peace.

All five warring nations agreed to join a League of Peace, the Iroquois Confederacy. The Peacemaker gave them a government and a constitution called "Kaianerekowa," today's Great Law. The clans that were to bind everyone together were also established at this time.

The Peacemaker planted a great white pine tree as a symbol of the League of Peace, a daily reminder of what the people had accomplished together. Then the tree was uprooted and deep beneath it ran a fast-flowing river. All the young men of the Five Nations were called to throw their weapons of war into that river, never to pick them up again. Ever after the people would act as one heart, one soul, and one mind for peace, prosperity, and righteousness. The eagle, the guardian bird of the Iroquois and the leader of all birds, would perch at the top the Peace Tree, representing eternal vigilance, and the four great white roots of the tree, leading in the four cardinal directions, would always lead the people back to the place where peace had come to the Five Nations.

For every peace chief there would be a clan mother, a female counterpart to keep the balance. Neither the fifty chiefs nor the fifty clan mothers of the confederacy would make the decisions; that power would rest with the people.

The fifty hereditary chiefs of the Five Nations gave the

Peacemaker a string of lake-shell wampum as a pledge of their loyalty to the Laws of the Great Peace. They promised to uphold the constitution of the Five Nations. When the Tuscarora Nation was adopted in 1722 the Five Nations became the Six Nations. There was no greater power than when these nations of the Iroquois Confederacy were united.

The Confederacy was like a longhouse with five doors but only one family. The Mohawk were the keepers of the eastern door, with the Seneca at the western door. In the middle the Onondaga were the Firekeepers at the capital of the League, the Central Council Fire.

Each nation sent a fixed number of chiefs to the Great Council held in Onondaga. They were chosen by the women from the leading families, with the official names of the chiefs being passed down to the next generation. Although each nation had its own council and council house, anything that affected the Confederacy itself had to be decided at the Great Council.

*

The Mohawk River flows east for most of its journey through central New York State. It links Molly Brant's homeland by way of a system of lakes, rivers, and creeks to Lake Ontario at Oswego and to the St. Lawrence via the Hudson River, Lake Champlain, and the Richelieu.

The foothills of the Adirondack Mountains lie north of the Mohawk Valley, and the melting snow from their peaks feeds the region's many creeks and streams. On the river's south side, along Schoharie Creek, is the country that has been home to the Mohawk people for thousands of years.

The area's easy access meant that throughout its early

history ownership of the fertile valley was the cause of frequent disputes. The first Europeans to settle the area were Dutch trappers and fur traders, establishing a post in 1614 on the Hudson River at Fort Nassau, within present-day Albany, New York. The first to buy land from the indigenous people in order to farm, the Dutch settlers became the Mohawks' friends and neighbours. Dutch merchants sold guns and ammunition to the Iroquois, helping to level the playing field in conflicts with the Huron from Quebec, who got guns from the French as early as 1609.

Looking for religious freedom, three thousand Germans from the Palatinate, a region in the southwestern part of that country, settled along the Hudson River in 1710, and a later wave of immigration brought more Palatines, who chose to settle along the Mohawk River at German Flats and Palatine Bridge. These settlers were later joined by the Irish, Scottish, and English.

Grain was the main crop grown by the European settlers. The Iroquois, an agricultural people with a deep reverence for Mother Earth, had already cleared much of the land, long before the arrival of the Europeans, for the growing of maize (corn) and its "sister" crops, squash and beans.

Arendt Van Curler (or Corlaer), a Dutch patriot who'd come to America from Holland in 1630, gained a reputation for dealing honestly and fairly with the Native people. He was the first superintendent and justice of the manor of Rensselaerwyck, located on both sides of the Hudson River, near present-day Albany. He was the colonial secretary until 1642 and the founder of Schenectady. The old Dutch towns of Albany and Schenectady were both known as Native trading centres.

The first covenant of friendship between the Dutch and the Iroquois was made around 1614. It was renewed a number of times over the years, and Van Curler developed it into a policy of lasting peace, a "covenant chain," as the English later called it, one that would remain until the American Revolution.

The Iroquois made a belt of shells known as the "Kuswhenta," the Two Row Wampum, in order to record the Treaty of Tawagonshi, that mutual agreement of peace, friendship, and respect between themselves and the Dutch (later, the British). It was an alliance between equals; neither was the subject of the other.

No written text exists of the friendship treaty. The exact date and terms were not important to the Iroquois because the Two Row Wampum and their oral traditions told the story. Wampum — either single strings or wider belts — was used as a pictorial record of the past, as an archive, and as confirmation of treaties and agreements.

Created by stringing beads of purple and white shells, usually made from saltwater quahog (clam) and whelk shells, onto plant fibres or sinew, wampum had no monetary value. When the Dutch and English later built factories in Boston to manufacture wampum, it became a commodity that the Natives would trade for. Even today, wampum is historically important.

3

Enter William Johnson

While she was growing up, many of Molly's neighbours were white settlers. One of those neighbours and a frequent visitor to the Canajoharie home of Margaret and Brant Kanagaradunka was William Johnson, who lived on the edge of Mohawk territory, west of Schenectady.

Johnson's uncle, Irish-born Peter Warren, a wealthy navy admiral living in New York, had bought thirteen thousand acres of land in the Mohawk Valley on the south side of the river, east of Schoharie Creek. He had hired his nephew William Johnson to manage the estate (called Warrensburg or Warrensbush), to run the farm, and to find settlers willing to lease the land.

Born in Ireland in 1715, William Johnson arrived in the Mohawk Valley in 1738, bringing with him a dozen Irish families prepared to settle in the area. Before long the twenty-three-year-old was clearing land, taking part in the fur trade with the Natives, and opening a store and a trading post. He built a house for himself on the north side of the Mohawk River, naming it Mount Johnson. William's nearest neighbour was another Irishman, John Butler, who lived with his two sons, John and Walter.

In 1739 William Johnson married Catherine Weissenburg. She may have been the daughter of a German Palatinate settler, although some sources say Catherine was actually a maid servant whom William had rescued while she was escaping her previous owner. If William Johnson married her, and there may have been a deathbed marriage (Catherine died in 1759), she was the only one of his three "wives" that he did.

The couple had three children that Johnson named as his legitimate heirs: Nancy/Ann, born in 1740, John (later, Sir John Johnson), born in 1742, and Mary/Polly, born in 1744.

William Johnson also had other children by Mohawk women. His eldest, born in the 1740s to an unknown Mohawk woman, was Brant (Kaghneghtago). His other son, William (Tagawirunte), later known as William of Canajoharie, was born in the 1750s and was the child of Molly's Aunt Caroline, Margaret's sister.

While Brant, the older boy (sometimes referred to as Young Brant or, more commonly, Brant Johnson), was said to have had a gentle nature, William of Canajoharie was an unruly youth with a violent temper. As was the Iroquois custom, both children were raised by their mothers or their mothers' families and may have lived with William Johnson when they were older.

In 1749, William, Catherine, and the children moved into a new house that William had built for them, a one-and-a-half-storey mansion of cut stone that he named Fort Johnson. It was located three miles west of today's city of Amsterdam, New York. Extensive gardens separated the house from the Mohawk River, and on the creek that flowed through the estate, Johnson built a gristmill.

From a plate in The Old New York Frontier *by Francis Whiting Halsey, Charles Scribner's Sons, 1901.*

Portrait of Sir William Johnson.

William Johnson was always on the lookout for opportunities to connect with the Mohawk people in order to increase his influence among them, and in 1746, New York governor George Clinton had put him in charge of Indian affairs. He had won the confidence of the Natives through his fair treatment of them, and the Mohawk came to prefer dealing with him than with the merchants and traders in Albany.

Molly and her brother Joseph may occasionally have visited Fort Johnson along with other Mohawk youths to participate in the outdoor games and events William Johnson liked to put on.

Johnson respected the Native culture. He learned the Mohawk language, joined them in their sporting events, and sometimes even wore Mohawk clothing. In return, the Mohawk adopted him as a brother, giving him the name Warraghiyageh, meaning "he who does much business."

At six feet in height, William Johnson was a tall man for his time and athletically built, with dark eyes and complexion. Described by some as "a man's man," William also enjoyed reading and used to order books from London for his personal library. The study of science, especially astronomy, was one of his many interests.

*

As early as 1713, a school, meant to serve all the local children, had been established at Fort Hunter, and it is likely that a number of Mohawk youngsters were among its students. William Johnson also persuaded some Mohawk parents to send their children to a school in Stockbridge, Massachusetts, which had been designed for both girls and boys. American theologian Jonathan Edwards was the teacher, and in his youth Molly's stepfather Brant had been a student there.

Molly herself may have received some formal education between 1740 and 1750 at a Church of England (Anglican) mission school. It has also been suggested that Molly may have later attended a private school for young ladies in Schenectady. Some of her biographers say that she was able to speak and write English fluently. Any letters of hers that have survived show excellent penmanship, but one cannot be certain the handwriting is Molly's.

When she was eighteen, in 1754 or 1755, Molly accompanied her stepfather and a delegation of other Mohawk elders, led by King Hendrick, to Philadelphia to discuss some questionable transactions involving the sale of land in the west to speculators from Connecticut. It would have been a chance for Molly to learn how business was conducted, although her role was likely one of an observer only. Iroquois women occasionally attended councils. Once their advice had been given, however, their participation was usually through a spokesman. It was the chiefs of the clans who were the orators, negotiating treaties and meeting with the chiefs of other nations. The women might be tasked with remembering what was said, what promises made.

Nonetheless, Molly's attendance at the council in Philadelphia is the first evidence of her involvement in political activity.

*

William Johnson played a significant role in the struggle between Britain and France for control of North America, known as the French and Indian War (1754–63) — part of the later Seven Years' War between Britain and France in Europe.

The French in Canada, wanting to limit Britain's influence along their frontier, had built a string of forts along the St. Lawrence from Quebec to Lake Erie and toward the forks of the Ohio River (at present-day Pittsburgh). The British set in motion a plan to stop the French from expanding right across the continent.

The Mohawk would have preferred to remain neutral in these wars between white men, but because of the trust they had in William Johnson, they reluctantly agreed to ally themselves with the local militia against the French. Because the British were unwilling to commit the troops needed to counter the

French on the North American continent, they depended on Johnson's Natives to make up for the shortfall in manpower.

Both the French and the British claimed title to the section of land that was used as a portage between Lake George and the Hudson River, a vital link in the system of waterways between Montreal and New York. Ironically, the land in question belonged to neither country, but to the Natives. The Europeans seemed to assume that if the land belonged to the Natives it was fair game.

Recently promoted to the rank of major-general, William Johnson led an army of British Colonials and Mohawk allies under the aged King Hendrick (Theyanoguen) to try to drive the French from the region by capturing the French fort at Crown Point.

As early as 1734 the French had built a large stone fortress at Crown Point, on the tip of a peninsula on the west side of Lake Champlain. The massive Fort St. Frédéric looked like a European castle, and as the first fort to be built along Lake Champlain, it had given the French control of the valley.

By the time Johnson's troops reached the southern tip of Lake George, in the fall of 1755, the French and their Canadian Native allies, intent on attacking British Fort Edward on the east bank of the Hudson River, were only an hour's march away.

The British quickly dug in, throwing together crude entrenchments of logs and stumps. The two forces met on September 8, 1755, in what became known as the Battle of Lake George. The French were narrowly defeated and their advance halted. Their commander, Major-General Baron Dieskau, was wounded three times, and the story goes that his life was finally saved by William Johnson.

Johnson was wounded by a musket ball that lodged in his hip. Theyanoguen had his horse shot from under him and was killed by a French bayonet.

After the battle, the Mohawk wanted to return to their homes, as was their custom, in order to grieve the loss of Theyanoguen and so many other brave warriors. Johnson tried in vain to convince them that the campaign to remove the French from their country had only just begun.

Unable to advance to Crown Point as he had planned, William Johnson had a fort built on the battlefield, on a bluff at the southern end of Lake George where it would command the waterway to Canada. The wooden fort had seventeen cannon mounted on its thirty-feet-thick walls. Johnson christened it Fort William Henry, after the two grandsons of King George II.

*

With old Fort St. Frédéric at Crown Point in a bad state of repair, the French set about building themselves another fort, this time at Ticonderoga, south of Crown Point at another narrows in Lake Champlain. *Ticonderoga* is a Mohawk word meaning "the land between the waters." The French called it Fort Carillon.

The year after the Battle of Lake George, William Johnson was made a baronet of Great Britain and received a gift of five thousand pounds from the British Parliament for his years of faithful service. He was also promised that his young son John would be knighted when the boy reached his twenty-first birthday. Although only about thirteen years old at the time, John Johnson and Joseph Brant had accompanied Sir William's 1755 expedition against the French at Lake George.

The following year, Sir William Johnson was appointed Superintendent of Indian Affairs for the Northern District.

4

Mistress of the Manor

Sir William Johnson's aide and secretary, Daniel Claus (1727–87), accompanied the Mohawk delegation to Philadelphia in 1755 when eighteen-year-old Molly Brant went along. Claus later reported that on the return trip, when they stopped in Albany, an English captain fell in love with Miss Molly Brant, who was "pretty, likely not havg. had the smallpox." Much of the Native population bore the scars of that disease, one of the curses brought to them by the Europeans.

Other biographers have written that Molly had a lighter complexion than one might expect of people of her race, implying that her father might have been white. There is no proof of that. One might also speculate that because her brother was of medium height, Molly may have been too. In the absence of any pictures of Molly Brant, physical descriptions of her can only be based on illustrations of other Mohawk women of her time.

Because of what we know about Molly Brant's character — she was intelligent, proud, persuasive in argument, and had strong leadership abilities, as well as remarkable stamina — one can imagine her having a regal bearing, taking long, confident strides when she walked, holding her head high, her back straight. And since Molly dressed in traditional Mohawk fashion, she would have worn moccasins on her feet, making little sound as she passed.

Daniel Claus was a prolific letter writer in his day, and he kept a diary and numerous journals of his travels. Historians have had to rely on his papers when no other records were available, so that much of what we read about Molly Brant today comes with Daniel Claus's personal bias. He was always supportive of Molly.

It wasn't long before Brant Kanagaradunka's attractive stepdaughter caught the eye of Sir William Johnson, Brant's friend and frequent house guest. There appears to have been a mutual attraction between them, and in 1759 Molly, who was twenty-three, and William, in his mid-forties, began living together as husband and wife. Sir William and Molly were never legally married in the eyes of British law, although it is possible that there might have been a traditional Mohawk marriage ceremony.

William's relationship with Molly served to further strengthen his ties with the Mohawk Nation. He seems to have taken under his wing her brother Joseph as well. William admired the young man, a quick learner, finding him modest and courteous. Some sources even suggest that Joseph might have been Johnson's biological son, based on the fact that they both had athletic builds and possessed similar personalities. There is no evidence to support this theory, however.

Joseph Brant's connection to Sir William, whose authority by this time extended to all the Natives north of the Ohio River, gained him admission to Moor's Indian Charity School in Lebanon,

Connecticut, in 1761, under the tutelage of Eleazor Wheelock, minister and teacher. Wheelock had established the school in order to recruit Christian missionaries from among its Native students. Here, Joseph learned to read and write English well.

With emphasis on Christian behaviour, the school also offered classes in Greek, Latin, and Hebrew. It was a long way from home for many of its Native students, however, and the Indian Charity School did not remain in existence for very long. When Wheelock decided to admit European students, he relocated his school to Hanover, New Hampshire. There it became Dartmouth College, with Wheelock as its first president.

By the time Molly Brant became part of the household at Fort Johnson, the stone manor house on the north bank of the Mohawk River, William's wife, Catherine, had died. Her two daughters, Nancy and Mary, continued to live in the family home, under the watchful eye of their governess. Their brother John had begun his education at the Academy in Philadelphia two years earlier, and he would remain there for a total of three years.

It is quite possible that William's two sons by Mohawk women — one of them Molly's Aunt Caroline — were occasional residents of their father's home. Catherine Weissenburg's elderly mother was also among those still living at Fort Johnson.

Molly appears to have been accepted by Sir William's two daughters without much difficulty. At twenty-three, she was only three years older than the eldest girl, Nancy. It was Nancy who had been in charge of the household since Catherine's death, a position that Molly took over from her.

But Nancy may have had other things on her mind. She was in love with Daniel Claus, who was at the time posted in Montreal as one of Sir William's agents. Perhaps Nancy was relieved to hand the management of the household over to Molly.

Daniel Claus had arrived in Canajoharie from Germany in 1750 and lived among the Mohawk, possibly with King Hendrick (Theyanoguen) himself, in order to learn the language and the Mohawk way of life, and from there the young man went on to become William Johnson's aide and personal secretary.

Daniel and Nancy were married in the front parlour at Fort Johnson on April 13, 1762, and because her new husband would be away much of the time, Nancy continued to live there. So, too, did her sister Mary, after her marriage in 1763 to Guy Johnson, a nephew of William's. Born in Ireland about 1740, Guy Johnson became Sir William's assistant in the Indian Department.

In September 1759, Molly gave birth to her first child. She and William named him after William's uncle and mentor, Peter Warren (also, possibly, after Molly's father, if indeed Margaret's husband was her father).

Molly was now wife, mother, and the manager of Sir William's household. William was often away for months at a time on business, and, as well as being the hostess to his many house guests, Molly found herself in charge of the servants, the slaves, and all the other employees. Fortunately, Molly relished her new role. She came to dominate the household and may even have assumed responsibility for the Department of Indian Affairs while William was away.

Fort Johnson was a busy place, more like a grand hotel than a home, and it seemed never to be without visitors. Governors and Native chiefs, military officials, and local people came by on a regular basis. In good weather, parties and games were often held outdoors on the grounds of the manor house.

Guests found Molly Brant to be intelligent and gracious. In turn, "Brown Lady Johnson," as she was sometimes called, was

Fort Johnson, near Amsterdam, New York.

always treated with great respect. She had long felt at home in both Native and European cultures, and this was no different.

For the most part, Molly continued to dress in Mohawk style. With her dark hair in a single long braid, she wore the traditional jacket, deerskin skirt, and leggings of her people. Like most influential Mohawk of the period who dressed in a combination of European and Mohawk styles, she may have begun to use European materials to sew her traditional clothing. She was by all accounts an excellent seamstress.

Although all of her children would be registered as Johnsons, Molly Brant kept her own name, thus ensuring her position in Iroquois society as a clan mother.

Fort Johnson, besides being a large, comfortable family home, also served as a fort and as an office for Indian Affairs.

Sir William employed staff to look after the gardens, a man to manage the farm, and had ten to fifteen black slaves who lived nearby with their families in private cabins. He had secretaries for his business affairs, and his own lawyer, physician, tailor, and blacksmith. Still acting as his uncle's agent, he was a wealthy landowner in his own right, as well as a farmer, a fur trader, a salaried army officer, and a colonel of fourteen companies of the militia. He also held a seat on provincial council.

Just after William's marriage to Molly, the Mohawk people had given him eighty thousand acres of land on the Mohawk River. He'd held the position of Superintendent of Indian Affairs for the northern division since 1756 and would keep it for the rest of his life.

The year that Molly went to live as Sir William's wife, the British planned to seize the French forts at Ticonderoga and Crown Point before advancing on Montreal. At the same time, British and American forces, together with their Mohawk allies, were planning to trek to Niagara and capture the fort.

The force was successful in ousting the French from Fort Niagara on July 25, 1759. This was the first time Molly's brother Joseph had been engaged in actual battle. The capture of Fort Niagara marked the end of French control of the western forts.

Back in August 1757, French general Louis-Joseph, the Marquis de Montcalm, had mustered his army at Fort Carillon at Ticonderoga and crossed Lake George to take Fort William Henry. They burned the fort Sir William Johnson had built two years earlier, and many British lives were lost when the fort's commander refused to surrender.

Now, two years later, as the British forces approached Fort Carillon, its French garrison fled, setting sail northward for Crown Point, but not before blowing up much of the fort. When the British reached Crown Point they found the French had abandoned it, too, after touching off barrels of gunpowder and blowing up Fort St. Frédéric.

British commander Jeffery Amherst ordered the building of a British fort at Crown Point, just west of old Fort St. Frédéric. His Majesty's Fort at Crown Point was the largest ever built in North America.

In the meantime, Amherst's plan to advance on Montreal was going ahead. The previous summer, 1758, the British capture of the French Fort Frontenac, a seventeenth-century fur-trading fort at the eastern end of Lake Ontario (in today's Kingston), had cleared the way up the St. Lawrence for the attack on Montreal.

On September 12, 1759, British general James Wolfe captured the city of Quebec, although both he and French general Montcalm, who had replaced Major-General Baron Dieskau as commander of French forces in Canada, died on the Plains of Abraham.

Remains of His Majesty's Fort at Crown Point, New York.

The bloodless capture of the city of Montreal in 1760, with the help of the Kahnawake Mohawks, would mark the end of the Seven Years' War on the North American continent.

*.

Molly Brant belonged to an Iroquois society in which women were listened to and respected. In the case of the senior women, their advice was even asked for. Unlike most European men, Iroquois men did not object to women who spoke their minds. It has been suggested that this may have been a source of irritation for Sir William, who disapproved of women taking part in political discussions, and that the couple's relationship was occasionally strained.

At times it appears that William tried to control Molly. When Molly was nearing the end of her first pregnancy, she had wanted to be at William's side in the campaign against the French at Niagara. She felt she might be able to use her influence to persuade the Seneca to side with the British, rather than with the French. But William sent her a message from Oswego, where the troops were gathering, telling her not to come. It was not in Molly's nature to take orders from any man. As an influential Mohawk clan mother, she knew she was indispensable to Sir William, and she was recognized as a competent and powerful woman in her own right. But on this occasion it appears that, heavily pregnant, she did as she was told.

Molly and Sir William's second child, daughter Elizabeth, was born in either 1761 or 1763. A third child, Magdalene, was born two years later. By this time the family had moved into a new home.

Nine miles back from the Mohawk River, and northwest of their earlier home, Johnson Hall was larger and more elegant than Fort Johnson. The two-storey Georgian frame house had two windows on either side of a central front door and five windows above on the second floor. The back of the house looked the same as the front. There were two fireplaces inside, a formal garden in the back along with two stone blockhouses, and a full cellar underneath. The main staircase of the house was impressive, and four large rooms opened off a grand central hall on both levels.

It was here, amidst the finest porcelain dishes, crystal wine glasses, and elegant furniture and linens, that Molly Brant, mistress of the manor, would prove her mettle as Sir William's hostess.

An Englishwoman who visited Johnson Hall gave this description of the gracious Molly: "She was quiet in demeanour, on occasion, and possessed a calm dignity that bespoke a native pride and consciousness of power. She seldom imposed herself into the picture, but no one was in her presence without being aware of her."

Johnson Hall, Johnstown, New York.

At the same time as Johnson Hall was being built, Sir William was seeing to the remodelling of his first home, Mount Johnson, where his daughter Nancy and son-in-law Daniel Claus would live. The couple renamed it Williamspark. Sir John, the son and heir, would live at Fort Johnson, and Sir William gave his other daughter, Mary, and her husband, Guy Johnson, an acreage on the Mohawk River. There they built a stone mansion that they named Guy Park.

No sooner had Sir William Johnson's family moved into Johnson Hall — in fact, the house was not fully completed — than the trouble that had been brewing in the west between the Natives and the white settlers in the Ohio Valley boiled over.

*

On May 15, 1763, Molly wrote a letter to her brother Joseph in Connecticut, where he was attending school, ordering him to return at once to Canajoharie. Up until that time, Joseph had been planning to go with a classmate, Charles Smith, to the Oneida village of Oquaga (also Ohoquaga) where they would work as interpreters. But Molly had learned that the Mohawk were not pleased with the education Joseph was getting or with his prolonged absence. He was one of their potential leaders and should be among his people. Besides, the situation in the Ohio Valley was worsening and Joseph, who had already been on a number of campaigns with Sir William, was needed at home.

By the time Molly's letter reached Joseph, the war with Chief Pontiac had begun, and both Joseph and Smith had decided Oquaga was too close to enemy territory for their own safety.

Deeply in debt after the expensive French and Indian War, Britain had developed new policies in regards to the Native

Americans. These included cutting back on the giving of presents to the Natives, seen by some British officials as bribery, and limiting the amount of ammunition and gunpowder the traders could sell to them.

If British officials were to offer money to the Natives for their help or their neutrality it would have been considered an insult to the Natives. But presents, be they clothing, hats, guns, or kettles, were quite acceptable; in fact, expected.

Sir William could see the danger in these new restrictions. His warnings were not taken seriously until hostile Natives began attacking British forts and settlements in the Great Lakes region and the Ohio Valley.

Chief Pontiac of the Ottawa nation, sensing that the British wanted the Natives driven from the country altogether, persuaded other western tribes — the Potawatomi and the Wyandot — to join the Ottawa in attacking Fort Detroit. By June 1763, when other groups of Natives, including the Shawnee and the Delaware, as well as the Seneca of the Iroquois Confederacy, joined the attacks, all but three of the twelve British posts on the Great Lakes had fallen.

Sir William recruited an army of settlers in the colony of New York in case Pontiac's forces came east. He ordered out the county militia, provided arms to the citizens of nearby Johnstown, armed his two stone blockhouses with cannon, and had a stockade built around Johnson Hall. For a while, it was an anxious time for everyone in the Valley.

By October, though, when the tribes that had sided with Pontiac realized that their former allies, the French, had lost the war with the British for good and would not be restoring their land to them, the siege of Fort Detroit ended. The Seneca came to Johnson Hall to make their peace with the British.

Thinking he could appease the Native population and stop the violence, King George III issued a Royal Proclamation on October 7, 1763. He declared a boundary between Native territory and the colonists' settlements, an invisible line extending down the length of the Appalachians, the range of mountains that runs through the eastern United States. White settlement was to be kept east of the line, contained between it and the coast. Many consider the Royal Proclamation of 1763 to be the first step on the road to the American Revolution.

5

Life at Johnson Hall

With the French and Indian War over, the future began to look a little brighter. Sir William believed that a firm alliance between the British and the Iroquois was possible and that he and Molly could settle in for some time together as a family.

In the fall of 1765 he sent his twenty-three-year-old son, John, off on a grand tour of the British Isles, in the company of Sir William's old friend, British MP Lord Adam Gordon. He'd be away two years.

The son of Catherine Weissenburg, John Johnson was a serious young man. He'd been educated in the local schools before going off to spend three years at the Academy in Philadelphia. Lord Gordon had reminded Sir William that he'd been promised a baronetcy for John after the youth's twenty-first birthday, and it was Gordon's opinion that John could do with a broader education, one that would rid him of any coarseness that might have resulted from his country schooling.

Earlier that same summer, Molly's brother, Joseph Brant, had married Margaret (Neggen Aoghyatonghsera), better known as Peggie, in a British-style wedding ceremony. The couple's first child, Isaac, named after Peggie's father, was born in Canajoharie.

Two other couples were married at the same ceremony as Joseph and Peggie — one unknown, and the other Brant (Kaghneghtago) Johnson and his white bride. Rumoured to have been the daughter of a wealthy Virginian, the girl had been captured years earlier by western Natives and was finally returned to Sir William. Because he was ill at the time, Sir William, Brant Johnson's father, did not attend the ceremony.

The home of Molly and Sir William Johnson was the scene of a dozen or more conferences and councils with the Natives between 1759, when the couple married, and 1774, the year of Johnson's untimely death.

Attended by hundreds of Native and government officials, supplies for these events had to be brought in by the wagonload. Long tables made of planks were set up outside for meals. Hogs and cattle were slaughtered, and great copper kettles of corn soup, a mainstay of the Natives' diet, were kept simmering over the open fires. The Natives would camp on the grounds around the manor house. One reason for building the grand central hall in the new house was to accommodate meetings such as these indoors in cases of inclement weather.

As an influential Mohawk clan mother and the partner of Sir William Johnson, Molly was in a good position to act as conciliator between the parties at the council meetings, occasionally persuading the more obstinate chiefs in the crowd to comply with Johnson's proposals. The Natives came to depend on her counsel, and Molly was always confident that Sir William had the best interests of her people at heart.

In an account of a visit he'd made to Johnson Hall, Judge Thomas Jones, Justice of the Supreme Court of the Colony of New York and a personal friend of Sir William's, described a typical day at the manor house where Molly and William hosted travellers from near and far. Life at Johnson Hall with Molly as household manager and chatelaine was most civilized:

> The gentlemen and ladies breakfasted in their respective rooms, and, at their option, had either tea, coffee, or chocolate, or if an old rugged veteran wanted a beef steak, a mug of ale, a glass of brandy, or some grog, he called for it, and it was always at his service. The freer people made, the happier was Sir William. After breakfast, while Sir William was about his business, his guests entertained themselves as they pleased. Some rode out, some went out with guns, some with fishing-tackle, some sauntered about the town, some played cards, some backgammon, some billiards, some pennies, and some even at nine-pins. Thus was each day spent until the hour of four, when the bell punctually rang for dinner, and all assembled. He had besides his own family, seldom less than ten, sometimes thirty. All were welcome. All sat down together. All was good cheer, mirth, and festivity. Some times seven, eight, or ten of the Indian Sachems joined the festive board. His dinners were plentiful. They consisted, however, of the produce of his estate, or what was procured from the woods or the rivers, such as venison, bear, and

fish of every kind, with wild turkeys, partridges, grouse, and quails in abundance. No jellies, creams, ragouts, or sillibubs graced his table. His liquors were Madeira, ale, strong beer, cider, and punch. Each guest chose what he liked, and drank as he pleased. The company, or at least a part of them, seldom broke up before three in the morning. Every one, however, Sir William included, retired when he pleased. There was no restraint.

Housework was not part of Molly's daily routine at Johnson Hall, although she may well have enjoyed tending the herb garden that grew on the estate. She had become an expert on the use of various plants for their healing qualities. Perhaps she also grew the Native medicines, sage, cedar, sweetgrass, and the sacred Indian tobacco, a combination of which, once dried, the Native people would burn to create smoke in order to cleanse themselves of any negative energy before healing could take place.

The Johnsons' house guests often sent Molly handwritten notes, thanking her for her hospitality. These notes were sometimes accompanied by gifts for her or the children. Obviously, Sir William's guests were well aware of the couple's children; they were not kept out of sight of the visitors.

Among the many guests at Johnson Hall in June 1765 were the Irish actor and dramatist William O'Brien and his bride, Lady Susannah Sarah Louisa Fox-Strangways (called Susan), the daughter of Britain's first Earl of Ilchester.

The couple had been forced to leave England for America because they had gotten married without the Earl's permission. Susan had been violently ill on the long voyage across the

Atlantic, and a chance to rest and relax at Johnson Hall must have been most appealing.

In her letters Susan wrote that her hostess, "Miss Molly Brown," was "a well bred and pleasant lady." The two women shared a few walks together on the estate, and, according to Susan, Molly "proved a delightful companion."

Another baby, daughter Margaret, named for Molly's mother, joined the Johnson family in 1767, and Molly's second son, George, was born the following year. The black walnut cradle in which she traditionally rocked all her babies to sleep was never empty for long.

It was around this time that Sir William, while frequently in pain from the hip injury he'd received at the Battle of Lake George, began to suffer prolonged periods of dysentery and other illnesses. In 1767, some of his Native friends took him to a secret spring near Fort Saratoga where the mineral water was believed to have medicinal properties. It appears to have had a good effect on Sir William, and after a time he returned home well enough to carry on with his duties.

Sir William spent a great amount of time trying to settle land disputes between the white settlers and the western Natives. During her husband's many absences, Molly managed the estate at Johnson Hall quite capably. Records show that she was responsible for ordering the materials needed for the running of the household. She may also have helped to purchase the presents that were given to the Natives attending the gatherings at Johnson Hall, and while Sir William was away she continued to see that her people received these gifts.

The Second Baronet of New York, Sir John Johnson, returned home from England in 1767 and went to live at Fort Johnson. There he began a love affair with blonde-haired Clarissa Putnam.

Of Dutch descent, Clarissa was from Tribes Hill, about three miles from Fort Johnson. Sir William let it be known that the girl, a farmer's daughter, was not up to his standards; she would never be a suitable mother for his grandchildren.

Molly, however, was more sympathetic and became John's confidante in the affair. Perhaps she recognized some similarity between his situation and her own. Although Sir William was not ashamed of his relationship with Molly and always treated her with the utmost respect, their children were not his legitimate heirs.

During the years they lived together, John and Clarissa had two children, William and Margaret (Peggy). The same age as her brother Joseph, Sir John was more like a younger brother to Molly than a stepson. They would remain close friends until the end of Molly's life.

*

European settlement continued to press westward into territory that had been reserved for the Natives by the Royal Proclamation of 1763. In the spring of 1768, Sir William convened a Great Council at Johnson Hall. Nine hundred Native leaders and many of their wives and children came to hear Sir William's proposal for a new boundary to protect their ancient hunting grounds.

After much discussion and the usual distribution of presents, the Native chiefs went home, confident that the proposal Sir William would present to the king's representatives at the provincial assembly would result in a firm land treaty.

That autumn a council was called at Fort Stanwix, an old fort at the head of the Mohawk River. Sir William's proposal was for a more permanent boundary than the one set out in the Royal

Proclamation of 1763. The new line was to be set as far west as the Natives would agree to, meaning they would have to give up many acres of their territory in order to reach the new agreement.

The Fort Stanwix Treaty line began in the west on the Ohio River, at the mouth of the Tennessee, near today's Paducah, Kentucky. It followed the Ohio in a northeasterly direction to Fort Pitt, present-day Pittsburg, Pennsylvania; and it ended at Wood Creek, near Fort Stanwix, east of Oneida Lake in New York State. The Natives had been very generous.

The lands the Natives sold for one thousand pounds are now part of the states of Kentucky, Tennessee, West Virginia, Pennsylvania, and New York. The Treaty of Fort Stanwix, one of the most important treaties ever signed between the Natives and the whites, was made official on November 5, 1768. The signatories were Sir William Johnson and the Six Nations chiefs, and the treaty was signed in the presence of representatives from New Jersey, Virginia, and Pennsylvania.

According to official accounts, the chiefs had requested that they receive the proceeds of the land sale in cash, since that was the quickest method, with the balance to be paid in six weeks.

The money was piled on a table, and the chiefs of each nation divided the shares amongst their people. It took all the rest of the day to complete the task. The following day, the Natives began to decamp and Sir William set out on his return journey to Johnson Hall, arriving home on November 9.

Under the new agreement the Mohawk towns of Canajoharie and Fort Hunter ended up on the British side of the line, but the Ohio River that the Natives called "The Indian River" would belong to the Six Nations forever.

*

In June 1769, Sir William was finally granted the patent for Kingsland, the eighty thousand acres of land on the north side of the Mohawk River that the Mohawk had given him ten years earlier as a token of their appreciation and trust. Because it was such a large grant, the king had to bestow the patent. It was here, between the East and West Canada Creeks, that Sir William had built his manor house and founded the village of Johnstown, which began as a site for the homes of the employees and staff of Johnson Hall.

One half mile east of his home, Sir William directed the construction of St. John's Anglican Church. He also had a school built in the village so that his children and those of his tenants could receive an education close to home.

However, Sir William's strenuous lifestyle continued to take a toll on his health, and by the late 1760s he was thoroughly exhausted and suffering terrible pain. Molly tended to his frequent bouts of illness as best she could, but the time came when even her Native medicines failed to help. Sir William spent the entire summer of 1770 in his bed. Later, he and Molly went away together to Castle Cumberland, a fortification on the southern shore of Sacandaga Lake in the former town of Caughnawaga, hoping a change of scene and the quiet location would restore Sir William's formerly robust health.

Two more babies were born to Molly and Sir William: Mary in 1771 and Susanna in 1772 (the same year as Molly lost a baby). Their eldest, Peter Warren, had been sent, at the tender age of seven, to Albany to study under Thomas Brown, an Anglican priest. From Albany, he left to attend a school in Schenectady run by the Anglican Church, but once a school was established in Johnstown, Peter came home.

The boy later went to Montreal for further education and to learn French. It must have been a relief to his mother to know that trusted friend Daniel Claus, husband of Sir William's daughter Nancy, would be keeping an eye on the youth while he was there. In 1773, Peter went to Philadelphia, where he would learn merchandising, apprenticed to a dry-goods merchant.

Peter wrote frequent letters home to his parents, sending greetings to his younger sisters, to his little brother, and to his friends. At only fourteen, the youngster may well have been homesick.

Always proud of his Mohawk heritage, Peter wrote to Molly asking her to send him some Native trinkets that he could show to anyone who might be interested. He also requested a book written in Mohawk, "for I am afraid I'll lose my Indian Toungue [*sic*] if I don't practice it more than I do."

From his father he requested a watch so that he'd always be on time. He did well at school and his teachers reportedly loved him. Peter became a sophisticated young man, quite at home in the company of his father's friends, playing his violin, or reading French, English, and Mohawk.

*

On a long hill that sloped down to the river in Canajoharie, Sir William had the Indian (or Upper Castle) Church built, and in 1769 it was close to completion. He wrote to the Society for the Propagation of the Gospel in Foreign Parts (SPG) in hopes of getting an Anglican missionary for the Natives. Sir William himself was a member of the SPG.

The Reverend John Stuart arrived in December of the following year and went to live in the parsonage at Fort Hunter, where he would be installed as chaplain at Queen Anne's Chapel. The stone parsonage, about one mile east of the fort, had been built in 1734 and is still standing today.

Born in Pennsylvania in 1740, Stuart was the son of Irish Presbyterian parents. Also serving as missionary to the Mohawk in northern New York, he preached his first sermon in the new church in Canajoharie on Christmas Day 1770.

Indian Castle Church. The only building associated with the Mohawks at Canajoharie that is still standing.

Stuart became a frequent guest at Sir William's and Molly's home. He also visited the home of Joseph Brant and his family, located just north of the Indian Castle Church, on the same hillside. Brant's second child, daughter Christina, had been born there in 1769. Now, Joseph's wife, Peggie, was dying of tuberculosis. She succumbed to the disease in March of 1771 and was buried in the old graveyard in Canajoharie.

In the spring of 1772, Joseph, now a widower, went to stay with Rev. John Stuart at Fort Hunter, where he worked as an interpreter for Stuart's church services. He also collaborated with Stuart to translate the Gospel of Mark and other writings into the Mohawk language.

In 1773, Sir John Johnson found himself a wife that his father would approve of. Sir William had prepared a list of women he felt were suitable for his son, but it is not known whether or not John's bride-to-be appeared on that list. She was Mary (Polly) Watts, the daughter of a wealthy New Yorker. The Watts family was reportedly one of the "best" families in New York, and the wedding was a lavish affair. Sir William's poor health, however, prevented him from attending.

That same year, Joseph Brant married Peggie's half-sister Susannah.

*

It wasn't long before white settlers began, once again, crossing the Ohio River, squatting on Native territory west of the line agreed on in the Fort Stanwix Treaty of 1768. The Natives were bent on protecting their land. They raided white villages and many were themselves murdered for standing their ground.

Sir William seemed barely well enough to resume his duties, but sensing a threat of total war, he called a council of Native nations together in 1774. Between six hundred and eight hundred Natives attended the council. The Six Nations wanted to assist their brothers in the west, but Sir William was urging them to "keep the war hatchet buried." It was up to the chiefs and clan mothers to keep the restive tribes from all-out war against the white settlers.

On July 11, a Seneca chief spoke to the assembly at Johnson Hall, laying out the Native grievances. On the second day of the council, when Sir William rose to address the crowd, he gave an impassioned speech that went on for two hours in the hot sun. With sweat pouring from his body, he praised the Natives for the control they had demonstrated thus far and for their continued allegiance to the king. He begged them to trust him to take their complaints to the government officials, assuring them the king would prevent any further intrusion onto their territory by the settlers.

At the end of his address, totally drained, Sir William asked for some time to rest indoors, out of the searing July heat, before the Natives gave their reply.

He collapsed inside his home, and within two hours Sir William Johnson, in his sixtieth year, was dead. Molly and his children were with him, as were Guy Johnson, his deputy, and Sir William's Mohawk son, William of Canajoharie. Molly urged William to ride at once to Fort Johnson to fetch Sir John.

The story goes that Sir John, in a vain attempt to reach his father's side before it was too late, rode his horse so hard that the unfortunate animal dropped dead from the effort.

Outside Johnson Hall, when the assembly of Natives heard that their trusted brother and protector, Warraghiyageh, had died, their grief was palpable, immediate and loud. For hours the summer night was filled with the sound of their wailing. And Molly, stricken with grief, knew that her life would never be the same.

6

Return to Canajoharie

One of Sir William Johnson's biographers, William Elliot Griffis, in his book *Sir William Johnson and the Six Nations* (Dodd, Mead & Co., New York, 1891), called the great man's death euthanasia. "By the grace of God he rested from his labours."

Other sources suggest that Johnson's death was the result of cerebral palsy. His passing was not entirely unexpected; Sir William's health had been deteriorating for some time.

On July 13, 1774, the Reverend John Stuart, Sir William's priest and friend, led the service and read the eulogy for the funeral of the first Baronet of New York at St. John's Anglican Church in Johnstown. More than two thousand mourners attended, including the governor of New Jersey and the justices of the Supreme Court.

Everyone wanted to pay his respects, not only the local settlers and the Mohawk people, but also delegates from other Native tribes and members of the Johnstown Masonic Lodge.

The chiefs of the Mohawk nation were seated in the church immediately behind the family, their presence at the service a special request of Sir William's. Such a huge crowd had joined the solemn procession from Johnson Hall to St. John's that most had to be satisfied with hearing the service through the open windows, while they stood outside.

The following day, the chiefs of the Six Nations held a memorial service of their own. Molly had asked her brother Joseph not to return to Fort Hunter right away. Guy Johnson — Sir William's nephew, son-in-law, and deputy in the Indian Department — let it be known that Sir William had recommended him to assume the role of Superintendent of Indian Affairs for the Northern Colonies. When he asked that Joseph Brant join him in the Indian Department as his interpreter, the Mohawk chiefs returned to their homes, satisfied that their trusted friend, Warraghiyageh, would have approved of the choice.

As Sir William's son and principal heir, Sir John Johnson inherited the bulk of his father's estate. He and his wife, Polly Watts, would leave Fort Johnson and take up residence at the manor house, Johnson Hall, where Sir John would look after his father's many tenants. Although he'd made it known that he had no interest in the Department of Indian Affairs, he did take over his father's office of major-general of the militia, where previously Sir John had been a captain.

Sir William's remains were laid to rest beneath the altar area of the Johnstown church, a church he'd built with his own money. When that original church was later replaced with another, Sir William's burial site ended up outside.

The Weissenburg children were listed in Sir William's will as his legitimate heirs. After the first in line, Sir John, came Sir William's two daughters by Catherine Weissenburg, and their spouses: Nancy and Daniel Claus, and Mary and Guy Johnson. Sir William provided for all thirteen of his children, including William of Canajoharie and Brant Johnson. To them he left specific bequests from among his horses and livestock.

Molly's eight children, described in the will as Sir William's "natural children by Molly Brant, my present housekeeper," each received a lot in the Kingsland Patent as well as other property, money, Sir William's personal clothing, and a quarter of all the slaves and livestock.

Molly had lost the love of her life, and although she was only thirty-eight, she would grieve for William all her remaining years. She was still a Mohawk clan mother, however, and she took her eight children (the youngest, Anne, just a year old) back to Canajoharie, where she owned several houses.

Sir William had been generous to Molly in his will, calling her his "prudent and faithful" housekeeper. Today's understanding of the word *housekeeper* is different from what it was in the eighteenth century, when it more often referred to someone who managed a household.

Sir William left Molly two hundred pounds in New York currency, lot number one in the Kingsland Patent, and a black female slave named Jenny, "the sister of Juba."

The house Molly chose for her family in Canajoharie surely must have been a large one because she and the children didn't arrive empty-handed. Many strong backs must have been enlisted to carry all her possessions from Johnson Hall. She and the family's four slaves (Jenny and Juba and two others) brought with them trunks of bedding and household goods, dishes and silver, feather beds and chairs, saddles, clothing that included jewellery, shoes, and hats, Peter's violin, even a bateau that may have been used to convey her goods across the Mohawk. Legend has it that Molly also brought with her two hundred silver broaches and three thousand silver crosses, items that she might trade or use as presents.

It is likely that Molly Brant used part of her inheritance to set herself up in a business in Canajoharie, operating a store from which she sold supplies, including rum, to the Natives.

During the three years that Molly and her family would spend in Canajoharie she sent her two eldest daughters, Elizabeth and Magdalene, ages about eleven and nine, to school in Schenectady. Fifteen-year-old Peter had left the Academy in Philadelphia when Sir William died, and he'd moved with the rest of the family to Canajoharie. He would leave shortly for England, in the company of other members of the extended Johnson family.

When Molly and her entourage arrived back in Canajoharie, Joseph Brant and his mother, Margaret, were still living in the village, as were Molly's Mohawk stepsons, William of Canajoharie and Brant Johnson, and Brant's wife. Molly's stepfather, Brant Kanagaradunka, had died sometime in the mid-1760s. No doubt Margaret, widowed for a third time, helped to raise Joseph's two children, Isaac and Christina.

Just as she had at Johnson Hall, Molly threw open the doors of her European-style home in Canajoharie to her Native and white friends. The Native people knew they could depend on her generosity, and she continued to hand out presents, reinforcing her influence among them. Her village store became the local gathering place, and soon the talk there began to focus more and more on the news that was coming in about the distressing situation among the white population.

Before his death, Sir William had been aware of the Colonials' dissatisfaction with the British government over what they saw as unfair taxes and over a series of "intolerable acts." After the Boston

Tea Party, a protest by the Colonials against British taxation in 1773, Boston Harbour was closed, and four regiments of British soldiers arrived in the town. The Colonials called a Continental Congress in Philadelphia in 1774 to discuss their grievances.

In April 1775, word came of battles in Lexington and Concord. The American Revolution had begun. In each of the thirteen colonies families found themselves divided in loyalty between the Colonial Patriots and the British Loyalists (or Tories, as they were scurrilously dubbed).

In May, a second Continental Congress was convened, and the Colonials established Committees of Safety, intent on getting the population to take an oath of loyalty to the Patriots' cause. If anyone refused, they would be jailed and their property seized.

Early in the pre-dawn hours of May 10, Patriot Ethan Allen, leader of the volunteer Green Mountain Boys, and Benedict Arnold, a colonel in the Connecticut militia, crossed Lake Champlain to join forces in a surprise attack on British Fort Ticonderoga, located at the southern end of the lake.

Fort Ticonderoga was in a state of disrepair at this time, and its British garrison was only fifty men strong. It and the big fort at Crown Point were the best-known British forts in the country. But both were undermanned, and both were easily captured. The taking of Fort Ticonderoga was one of the first victories for the Colonials in the Revolution.

After Ticonderoga, Arnold and Allen moved north toward Canada, into the Richelieu River, intending to raid Fort St. Jean. They made an initial assault on the fort on May 18, before returning to Fort Ticonderoga.

Alerted to the attack, General Guy Carleton, commander-in-chief of British forces in Canada and governor of Quebec, moved his headquarters from the town of Quebec to Montreal and began reinforcing the garrison at Fort St. Jean.

As the situation worsened and word came of atrocities toward those Americans who were loyal to the king, Molly and Joseph Brant realized they might be forced to choose sides, in spite of the Natives' desire to remain neutral. Molly knew that Sir William, although he might understand the complaints of the Colonials, would never have turned his back on the king.

Sir William had been confident that as long as the Natives remained under the influence of Rev. John Stuart and other missionaries of the Anglican Church (the Church of England), they would stay on the side of the British against the rebel Colonials. Other missionaries, such as the Reverend Samuel Kirkland, a Presbyterian missionary from New England, had worked among the Oneida and Tuscarora, and when the Revolutionary War erupted, many from those tribes chose to side with the Patriots.

Guy Johnson, provisional Superintendent of Indian Affairs, was the leader of the Loyalists in the vast Tryon County, the boundaries of which extended north to the St. Lawrence, south to the Pennsylvania border, and west to Lake Erie.

Most of the residents in the Mohawk Valley were loyal to the powerful Johnson family. Its members included Sir John, Colonel Guy Johnson, Colonel Daniel Claus, Molly Brant and her eight children, Joseph Brant, and Sir John's half-brothers, William of Canajoharie and Brant Johnson. Important local men such as Nicholas Herkimer and Philip Schuyler were on the side of the Patriots, however, and their numbers were continuing to grow. Because Herkimer and Schuyler had been old friends of Sir William's, Molly felt she was safe.

As Patriot activity increased and the Tryon County Committee of Safety went about harassing Loyalists, Guy Johnson and his followers recognized the danger they were in. When Guy got wind of a rebel plan to arrest him and his staff, he increased security around Guy Park, his beautiful home on the banks of the Mohawk River.

During this time, a letter intended for the Oneida and signed by Joseph Brant and other sachems fell into the wrong hands. It requested that the Oneida come to help the Mohawks protect Guy Johnson. When the Rebels got hold of the letter, they were quick to assure Johnson that he was perfectly safe. Guy Johnson didn't know whom he should believe.

Then, a letter came for him from General Thomas Gage, commander of British forces in America during the early days of the Revolution. Gage ordered Johnson to gather as many Iroquois warriors as possible and go to Canada, where they would join forces with General Carleton's troops for a descent on the Rebels in New England. Along the way, he was to try to win allegiance for the British from other members of the neutral Iroquois Confederacy. When word of the order reached Joseph Brant, he, too, began gathering supporters, both white and Native, to join the expedition to Canada.

Using as an excuse his attendance at a council of Natives that was to take place in Oswego, New York, Johnson left Guy Park. As soon as the conference was over he intended to head to Canada. And he would not be alone.

Among those going with Johnson were one hundred and twenty whites and ninety Natives; Guy's pregnant wife, Mary, and their three children; Daniel Claus, his wife, Nancy, and their child; John Butler and his eldest son, Walter (leaving the rest of his family behind); Peter Warren Johnson, who was not yet sixteen; William of Canajoharie, who was game for anything; Captain John Deserontyon, a Mohawk chief from Fort Hunter; and Joseph Brant, who also left behind a family.

On May 31, 1775, the Johnson family and their followers set off, forming a long line of bateaux, moving up the Mohawk. No doubt Molly was among the crowd waving farewell from the banks of the river. A number of the travellers would never return. And from now on Molly would have to be satisfied with infrequent letters from her soldier son.

Molly Brant stayed behind in Canajoharie with her remaining brood, as did Brant Johnson, and, in Fort Hunter, Rev. John Stuart. Sir John Johnson chose to stay behind, too, at his beloved Johnson Hall, where his wife Polly was expecting. He had the idea that if he stayed out of it, the trouble would blow over, and that one day life as he knew it would resume. He couldn't have been more mistaken.

By the time the council at old Fort Ontario in Oswego ended, a few hundred warriors had accepted the war hatchet offered them by Guy Johnson, signifying their support of the king's forces. But they had accepted it grudgingly. Most of the Natives attending the conference (according to Johnson, there were 1,458) took their presents and returned home. Only a small group of warriors carried on with him to Montreal.

Just hours before Guy Johnson and his followers were to strike out from Oswego for Montreal, his wife, Mary, who was with him on the trek, died during childbirth. It was a sorrowful group that began the journey north on July 11, 1775. Many of the travellers had known Sir William's youngest daughter since she was a child, and they mourned her loss. Mary's three small daughters continued on toward Montreal with their father, no doubt comforted by their mother's sister Nancy and their uncle, Daniel Claus.

Arriving in Montreal on July 17, Guy Johnson and the officials in his party were surprised at the cool reception they got from the governor of Quebec, General Guy Carleton. Once a rival of Sir William Johnson's for control of the fur trade — Carleton on the French side, Sir William on the British — the governor was not a fan of the Johnson family. He'd long been jealous of the empire Sir William had carved out for himself in New York State, and resentful of Johnson's influence on the Indian Department in Quebec. Now he opposed the plan to use the Iroquois against the Colonials in the Revolutionary War, preferring they remain neutral.

Johnson informed Carleton of General Gage's instructions to him. But there was to be no joint march on the Rebels in New England; the Rebels were poised to invade Canada.

A conference with Canadian Natives and Johnson's Mohawks was held in Montreal July 26–29, and at that time Carleton assured the Iroquois that if they co-operated with the British they would get their land and property back when the war ended. But contrary to what Guy Johnson had expected, Carleton had no intention of using the Natives anywhere, except in the defence of Canada.

Those Natives who had followed Guy Johnson settled themselves into several encampments outside Montreal. Joseph Brant was part of a Native group allowed to go out on small scouting expeditions as far as Fort St. Jean and to engage in minor skirmishes.

While the rebel invasion was underway, Joseph was stationed near St. Jean, but he was confused over Carleton's lack of confidence in the Natives. Why was the man holding them back? In a small battle near Fort St. Jean on September 16, the Natives defeated the Rebels, successfully slowing the enemy's advance.

*

In August 1775, Lieutenant-Colonel Tench Tilghman, a secretary and aide to General George Washington (commander of the Continental Army), travelled to Canajoharie to urge all Mohawk chiefs to attend a conference to be held at German Flats.

Molly Brant was among the Natives who came to the conference, and Tilghman paid particular attention to her. In his memoirs he later wrote, "She saluted us with an air of ease and politeness ... one of the company that had known her before told her she looked thin and asked her if she had been sick, she said sickness had not reduced her, but that it was the Remembrance of a Loss that could never be made up to her, meaning the death of Sir William." Tilghman also made note of how Molly was dressed, "in Indian style but with the finest cloth."

Tilghman's next words were more prescient. "The Indians pay her great respect and I am afraid that her influence will give us some trouble, for we are informed that she is ... entirely in the Interests of Guy Johnson who is in Canada."

7

Mohawk Valley Exodus

"Canada," adapted from the Huron-Iroquois word *kanata*, meaning village, was the name the people of New France gave to the land around the settlement that later became Quebec City. After the British victory on the Plains of Abraham, the country north of the St. Lawrence River and the Great Lakes became Quebec, named for its capital.

General George Washington, like many other Colonials, considered the Quebec Act, passed by British Parliament in 1774, a threat to American expansion. Among other provisions, the act extended the boundaries of the Province of Quebec westward to include Ohio territory, as well as the land between the Great Lakes and Hudson Bay. The Americans saw the capture of Quebec as crucial, and early in the Colonials' fight for independence, Congress decided to attack its neighbour to the north on two fronts.

On June 27, 1775, the Continental Congress instructed an American army under Major-General Philip Schuyler and his deputy, Brigadier-General Richard Montgomery, to sail from Crown Point and invade Quebec through the Lake Champlain corridor. Once they had captured Fort St. Jean on the Richelieu River (the fort was Quebec's main defensive point south of Montreal), the plan was that they would move on to take Montreal itself. A second army under Colonel Benedict Arnold, after first trekking through the wilderness of Maine, would mount a surprise attack on the city of Quebec.

The American siege of Fort St. Jean began on September 16, 1775. It would last a total of six weeks. During this time, on October 18, an American detachment forced the surrender of Fort Chambly, located farther to the north.

Patriot Ethan Allen, commander of the Green Mountain Boys, was part of Major-General Philip Schuyler's military expedition. While the siege of Fort St. Jean was going on, Allen set out for the St. Lawrence River and Montreal. But before he and his men could reach the city they were met by a British detachment led by Walter Butler of the King's 8th Regiment and sixteen-year-old Peter Warren Johnson, Molly Brant's eldest son, of the 26th Regiment of Foot.

Thinking his rebel force outnumbered, Allen surrendered. He was taken prisoner and subsequently sent to England. Allen would be held until May 1778, at which time he would be part of an exchange of prisoners. The officer who received Ethan Allen's sword in surrender, on September 25, 1775, was none other than Peter Warren Johnson.

In September 1775, Major John Campbell arrived in Montreal from England, ready to take over Daniel Claus's position in the Indian Affairs Department. Governor Carleton wanted to have more direct control over the Department of Indian Affairs in Montreal.

Portrait of Joseph Brant. Toronto Reference Library, Baldwin Room. JRR 158 Cab II. "Joseph Tayendaneaga, Called the Brant." Artist, John Raphael Smith, engraved from original by George Romney, 1776.

As if that weren't bad enough, Governor Carleton informed Guy Johnson that he had no authority over any Natives in Quebec.

After learning that the Iroquois were not to fight outside Quebec, some of Guy Johnson's warriors left Montreal. One of these was William of Canajoharie, who arrived back in the

Mohawk Valley boasting of all the Rebels he had killed while he was away. This was typical of his bluster.

Tired of waiting in Montreal, and stung by Carleton's rejection, Guy Johnson, Daniel Claus, and Joseph Brant decided to leave Canada and sail to England, where they hoped they could have Carleton's arrangements overturned.

In London, Guy Johnson wanted to see the colonial secretary and have the position of Superintendent of Indian Affairs, which he'd assumed after the death of Sir William, made official, and Joseph intended to lay the Natives' grievances before the British Parliament. Daniel Claus was hopeful of a new position to replace the one he'd just lost to John Campbell.

The British commander of the besieged Fort St. Jean, Major Charles Preston, finally surrendered the fort on November 3, 1775. It had been a long siege, but by holding out as long as they had against the American troops, the British had slowed the American offensive. Montgomery had been hoping to arrive below the walls of Quebec City by mid-October; instead it would not be until early December, and he would have only a small portion of his men with him.

With the surrender of Fort St. Jean, Governor Guy Carleton ordered the evacuation of the city of Montreal, leaving it defenceless. Carleton, disguised as a peasant, escaped the city in a whale boat, heading for Quebec. He had already sent his wife and three children to safety in England.

Fortunately, our party of fifteen Loyalists had left Montreal by this time, sailing on the ship *Adamant* from Quebec City on November 11, 1775. Two days later the Americans would take possession of Montreal.

Included in the group bound for England were Guy Johnson's three motherless daughters, Daniel and Nancy Claus and their child, and Peter Warren Johnson. While he was in England, Peter would be commissioned as ensign in the 26th Regiment, as a reward for "capturing" the leader of the Green Mountain Boys.

At the last minute, John Hill (Oteronyente), a Mohawk from Fort Hunter, had arrived in Montreal with a message from Sir John Johnson for General Carleton. The Natives immediately persuaded Hill to accompany Joseph Brant to England where the two would act as their peoples' ambassadors in London.

*

American colonel Benedict Arnold's troops had left Maine for Quebec in September, only to discover that the maps they were following were outdated and inaccurate. The army began running out of food, and it was further hampered by floods and an early snowfall. By the first week of November they were a month behind schedule, and Arnold had lost half of his men.

The garrison within the walled city of Quebec was woefully inadequate, and General Carleton wondered if he could count on better support from its citizens than he'd received in Montreal, where the Americans had been welcomed more or less with open arms.

On December 3, Montgomery arrived in Quebec City with his remaining three hundred men, ready to join forces with Arnold's troops. Carleton is said to have burned the letter Montgomery sent him demanding surrender.

For weeks the Americans kept up a bombardment of the walled city's formidable defences, to little effect. Then, at two o'clock in the morning on December 31, in a blinding blizzard, the firing of two rockets signalled an American attack on the city from two different directions.

Carleton had earlier arranged to have a series of barricades built, and when Montgomery's forces reached Lower Town and came up against the first barricade, Montgomery was shot through the head. His men fled into the swirling snow.

Arnold's seven hundred men also managed to get into Lower Town, but Arnold was wounded when Carleton brought a small force up behind them. The Americans retreated, and for the rest of the winter Arnold and his remaining men found shelter in some farmhouses outside Quebec City, recuperating and waiting for reinforcements.

Back in Montreal, the American forces found their occupation of the city turning sour. The local citizens were becoming hostile, and their own army, many of whose men were sick, was threatening mutiny.

When the ice went out of the St. Lawrence River in the spring, and British ships arrived bearing reinforcements, Colonel Benedict Arnold admitted defeat and retreated down the Richelieu to Lake Champlain. Many of his men, and Arnold himself, were sick with smallpox. They stopped in Crown Point, where the sick were shipped to hospital. On May 9, 1776, the Americans abandoned Montreal.

*

Even though so many of her extended family had left the Mohawk Valley, Molly Brant remained in Canajoharie, listening to the talk in her store and keeping an eye on her white neighbours. But Molly herself was being watched. It was no secret where her loyalties lay.

She was suspected of hiding Loyalists who were trying to escape the bands of Patriot vigilantes, of providing the Loyalists with food and shelter, and even of sending arms and ammunition to those fighting on the side of the British. Molly remained firm in her belief that the best interests of the Six Nations could be served by siding with the British. They were the ones who would help the Natives preserve their homeland. She continued to remind her people that Sir William would want them to stay loyal to the king. By this time, Molly's mother, Margaret, may have already left Canajoharie for safety with her relatives in Cayuga.

Both sides in the conflict were courting the Natives. During the French and Indian War the Mohawk had joined the British and Americans in fighting the French, and now they were being asked to choose between their two former allies. For many it was a question of which side would preserve their autonomy. One Mohawk sachem, Little Abraham of Canajoharie, managed to remain neutral and uninvolved throughout the entire Revolution.

On the other side of the Atlantic, in London, Joseph Brant got his audience with the colonial secretary, Lord George Germain, and he made his appeal, protesting that the British had done nothing to protect Mohawk land, while many brave warriors had died. He was told that if the Mohawk helped thwart the Rebels' cause, their land claims would be settled once the war was over.

The handsome thirty-three-year-old Native made quite a splash in London. Feted as a Mohawk "chief," he had his portrait painted by acclaimed British artist George Romney. He was even initiated into the Falcon Lodge of the Order of Masons, something that would never have happened at home. (Many years later, in 1797 in Brant's Town, Joseph Brant and some white associates founded Lodge No. 11, one of the earliest Masonic lodges in Upper Canada.)

It was also during this London visit that Joseph Brant was interviewed by James Boswell for a July 1776 article in *London Magazine*. In the article the writer calls Brant the grandson of one of the Four Kings "who'd visited Queen Anne in 1710." Since the Mohawk term for grandfather also refers to great and great great grandfather, as well as the brother of those grandfathers, it is possible that Joseph was some sort of relative.

Joseph came away from his visit to London convinced that the British would uphold their end of the bargain and protect his people.

Guy Johnson was affirmed in London as Superintendent of Indian Affairs, with the same powers and authority as Sir William had had, although he would have no authority over the Natives in Quebec. That would be Major Campbell's mandate.

In early June 1776, Joseph Brant, John Hill (Oteronyente), and Guy Johnson sailed for home, leaving Daniel Claus and young Peter Warren Johnson behind. Claus had decided to stay in London, still hopeful of another appointment, and Peter would be returning to America with the rest of his regiment.

Because of the very real threat of rebel privateers at sea, the ship carrying Brant, Oteronyente, and Johnson was armed, and it sailed in a protective convoy, part of a flotilla taking arms and supplies to British forts in New York. They were fired on before their arrival in British-held Staten Island on July 29, 1776. At the time, New York City was occupied by the Rebels.

Two months earlier, in the Mohawk Valley, Sir John Johnson had hurriedly buried all his important papers and valuables. He'd received news (possibly from Molly Brant herself) that the Tryon County Committee of Safety with whom he'd struggled for a year was on its way to arrest him. Leaving behind his pregnant wife, Polly, and young son William, he fled Johnson Hall, heading north into the Adirondack Mountains.

He took 170 friends and followers with him, but after ten days, with the food supply running out, some gave up and went home. High in the mountains, living on berries and leaves and weak from hunger, the group was forced to abandon the three-pound cannon they were dragging with them. They managed to reach Montreal on June 18, 1776.

Back in the Mohawk Valley, when Major-General Philip Schuyler discovered that Sir John had escaped, he had the man's family arrested and taken to Albany, where they were placed under house arrest. The Rebels then looted Johnson Hall.

Meanwhile, in Montreal, Governor Carleton commissioned Sir John Johnson lieutenant-colonel and authorized him to raise a regiment that became known as the "Royal Greens," the King's Royal Regiment of New York.

That winter, Polly Johnson found a way to escape from the house in Albany where she was being held. She, along with little William and a black servant, set out for New York City. Disguised as simple country folk, they managed to get a horse and carriage, and they followed the Hudson River to the city. There, Sir John, who had returned to New York from Montreal by sea, found them. Sadly, it appears Polly's newborn baby died somewhere along the way.

A more colourful version of this story recounts how Sir John found Polly and the servant struggling through deep snow in an effort to reach him, the new baby dead in her arms. However it happened, when the time came for Sir John to return to Quebec with his regiment, he took his family with him. Until the war was over, the Johnsons would live in Lachine in a house with a view of the rapids. The couple would have many more children.

*

Back home again after many months in England, Joseph Brant found much had changed. The Rebels had not been able to keep Montreal, and Brigadier-General Montgomery had been killed outside Quebec City. The Declaration of Independence had been adopted by the Continental Congress on July 4, 1776.

Joseph was eager to deliver to his people the message he'd received from the king through the colonial secretary: They must be ready to fulfill their promise and co-operate with the British armies in Quebec and New York.

But on Staten Island, both he and Guy Johnson, along with the rest of the Indian Department, were ordered to put themselves under the command of British general William Howe. Howe, who had replaced General Thomas Gage as commander of the British forces in America, was planning an assault on New York City.

By the time they took New York, on September 15, it was too late in the season for Howe's army to continue its campaign, and Joseph was permitted to return to Native country. Accompanied by Gilbert Tice, a Mohawk Valley Loyalist who had been with him in London, Joseph set off. The two were in disguise because the countryside was swarming with enemy scouts and patrols. They crossed the Hudson River on November 16 and struck out cross country.

After a quick reunion in Oquaga, where earlier Joseph's wife and children had gone to live in the home of Susannah's father, Joseph hurried on to Niagara, ready to receive further instructions from John Butler. Before he'd left Montreal, Governor Carleton had made John Butler deputy agent in charge of Indian Affairs at Niagara, in Guy Johnson's absence. Butler had hoped he'd be able to return to his own home in the Mohawk Valley, but it was no longer safe to do so.

John Butler agreed with Governor Carleton's refusal to allow Natives to participate in the war, at least until the British armies were ready to move. He was trying to follow the governor's order to keep them under control, and he refused to let Joseph call a Native council at Fort Niagara.

Undeterred, Joseph Brant travelled back and forth between Niagara and the Mohawk Valley, trying to drum up Native support for the British. The Oneida and some of the Tuscarora rejected his urgings outright. He did find some support among the downtrodden Loyalists who'd sought protection in Oquaga, and it was from this group that Joseph raised one hundred men, both Native and Loyalist, for Brant's Volunteers. In retaliation for its inhabitants' support of the British, in 1779 the Patriots would burn the village of Oquaga to the ground.

In early August, Joseph Brant got his chance to be involved in the conflict. Butler sent him to Oswego, where he was to join forces with British lieutenant-colonel Barry St. Leger's troops, which were attempting to retake Fort Stanwix from the Rebels (in present-day Rome, New York) in central New York State. In Oswego, Brant's Volunteers met up with Butler's Loyalist Rangers and Sir John Johnson with the King's Royal Regiment of New York.

At home in Canajoharie, Molly Brant had been watching the movements of one of her neighbours in particular, General Nicholas Herkimer. She had determined that he was preparing to take the entire Tryon County militia to aid in the defence of Fort Stanwix. Acting on this intelligence, Molly sent Native runners on August 5, 1777, to warn her brother that the rebel militia, some eight hundred strong, was on its way.

On August 6, already engaged in laying siege to the fort, St. Leger acted on this intelligence and ordered Sir John Johnson, Joseph Brant, and Butler's Rangers to intercept the approaching militia.

The Loyalist troops chose a ravine near the Oneida village of Oriska, about six miles from the fort, for an ambush. In the bloody encounter that followed there were many casualties. General Herkimer himself died of wounds received in the battle. Some sources report that William of Canajoharie was killed that day; others say he killed a man in a bar fight later on and disappeared, never to be heard from again.

Back at the fort, St. Leger heard the gunfire from the battle, and he sent a detachment to assist Sir John's troops. While this was going on, a group of Americans slipped unnoticed from the fort, found the Loyalist Natives' unprotected camp, and stole whatever they could from it — supplies, clothing, and blankets. They managed to get back inside the fort without being caught.

The siege of Fort Stanwix, which was part of a larger campaign at Saratoga, New York, lasted most of August. When St. Leger heard three thousand Rebel troops were on the way, he abandoned the siege of the garrison and returned to Oswego. Both sides claimed victory, but because St. Leger had finally withdrawn, the Americans decided that they had won.

After what became known as the Battle of Oriskany, the Six Nations no longer talked of neutrality, although not all of them sided with the British — and that fractured the Iroquois Confederacy. The Loyalist Natives destroyed the Oneida village, home to those who'd sided with the Americans and had joined Herkimer's militia.

The Tryon County Committee of Safety was convinced that Molly Brant had sent information about the militia's troop movements to the British. She was now in mortal danger. She and her children were ordered to leave Mohawk Valley or face imprisonment in Albany. Before she left, Molly was subjected to verbal abuse, her cattle were stolen, and her overseer was murdered.

A group of men claiming to be looking for Joseph forced their way into her home one night and searched it. One of her children, most likely Margaret, who would have been about seven at the time, later testified to this terrifying incident.

The Oneida, seeking their own revenge for Oriska, set about burning Mohawk homes and villages. At the slightly more affluent Fort Hunter, they stole household furniture and even made off with crops and farm implements. By the time the looters entered the almost-abandoned village of Canajoharie, they found no one home at Molly's house. Leaving behind most of her treasured possessions, she and the children had fled.

8

Life at Fort Niagara

The remaining Native inhabitants of Fort Hunter had earlier begun to leave the Mohawk Valley and head for Canada. By the autumn of 1777, many had found shelter at Lachine and nearby Montreal. The Rebels arrested the Fort Hunter pastor, Rev. John Stuart. They confiscated his farm and stole his possessions, and he was parolled within the city of Schenectady.

It had taken a second unwelcome nighttime visit by strangers to her home in Canajoharie to convince Molly that she had to get out while she still could. Her brother Joseph may have arrived just in time to help her and the children make their escape.

After Barry St. Leger's troops had withdrawn from the siege of Fort Stanwix, they had returned to Oswego and from there gone on to join General John Burgoyne's army. Thinking they might do the same, Joseph Brant and some of his men made their way through the woods to the British camp.

When Joseph realized the dire circumstances of Burgoyne's nearly six thousand troops, he changed his mind about joining them. The British troops were demoralized and running out of supplies. Led by the over-confident Burgoyne, who had thought a victory would be easy, the troops had marched from Quebec, expecting to meet up with British general William Howe's army. Howe's troops were supposed to come north from New York City. But Howe's army never came. It was late in the season and they'd gone off in another direction.

Now Burgoyne's men were hemmed in by the forces of American general Horatio Gates. Although they had tried several times without success to break though enemy lines that September, disaster seemed imminent. Rather than risk capture himself, Joseph Brant had second thoughts and returned to Canajoharie.

No sooner had Molly and her family left than looters broke in and ransacked her house, carrying off her treasures, including ornaments and jewellery. In later writings, Daniel Claus maintained it was the vengeful Oneida who destroyed Molly's home. But renegade Rebels must have had a hand in it, too. The daughter of one of the Rebel leaders was later seen parading around in a formal silk gown belonging to Molly or one of her daughters.

Peter Deygart, chairman of the Tryon County Committee of Safety, had urged the Oneida Natives to make up for whatever they'd lost in Oriska by looting the homes of the Mohawk. "If you lost one cow," he said, "take two."

When Molly, her children, and the family's four faithful servants reached Onondaga, near present-day Syracuse, New York, the resident Natives invited them to stay. But Molly insisted on pressing on to Cayuga, where she had some distant relatives. It was there, near Lake Cayuga, one of the Finger Lakes in north-central New York State, that the family settled into the home of one of the principal chiefs.

Molly got word of British general Burgoyne's defeat and the surrender to the Americans at Saratoga in October 1777. It was a turning point in the war. France would soon enter the conflict on the side of the Colonials, in retaliation for its defeat in the French and Indian War, and in April 1779, Spain, too, would assist the Americans by providing financial aid.

With news of Burgoyne's surrender, many Iroquois began to doubt the wisdom of staying loyal to the king, thinking they should make their peace with the Rebels and reclaim their former neutrality. Molly Brant seized the opportunity to speak out publicly, declaring her own support for the Crown.

At an Iroquois council meeting that Molly attended at Onondaga, the Iroquois Central Council Fire in 1777, Sayengaraghta, a Seneca chief, addressed the Natives, urging them to espouse neutrality.

Molly rose to her feet and boldly denounced the chief. Her voice breaking and close to tears, she reminded him of his friendship with Sir William, of how Sir William had been the one who had arranged for all the presents from the king. What had the Americans ever done for the Natives, she asked, except steal their land? Hadn't Joseph Brant just told them that the king had promised to return that land when the war was over?

Some sources say that Molly tried to persuade the Natives to make an official declaration of war against the Americans. That didn't happen, but Molly spoke with such passion that she convinced the Five Nations (now without the support of the Oneida) to stick to the agreement they'd made with Sir William to honour the Covenant Chain. Afterward, she was promised retaliation for the attack on her home.

As Sir William Johnson's widow, Molly had even more influence with the Natives than she'd had while she lived at Johnson

Hall, a fact not lost on the British authorities who were about to ask for her assistance.

Molly Brant was still in Cayuga when she began receiving urgent messages from Major John Butler, who was stationed at Niagara as deputy Indian commissioner in charge of keeping the goodwill of the Natives. Throngs of Natives fleeing for their lives were pouring into Fort Niagara, the fort Sir William's forces had seized from the French in 1759. If anyone could help keep the Natives under control, Butler knew, it was Molly Brant. A friend of the Johnsons and formerly a trusted agent in the Indian Department under Sir William, Butler had also been appointed a guardian of Molly's children.

Molly was torn. She hated to appear ungrateful to her Cayuga hosts, but her people in Niagara needed her. Late in 1777 she found a way to leave without any hard feelings, and she set out for Niagara with the children and the family's servants.

Although John Butler had promised Molly a house of her own in Niagara when he urged her to come, it's more likely that she spent that first winter crowded in with Joseph and his family, who he'd earlier brought to safety from Oquaga. In a letter Joseph wrote to Daniel Claus on January 23, 1778, he states, "My sister and her family joins me to give our best compliments to Mrs. Claus."

Molly's mother, Margaret, was also in Niagara, as were Molly's stepson Brant Johnson and his wife and their two fair-haired daughters. Brant Johnson had become a lieutenant in the Indian Department, serving with Butler's Rangers.

The dilapidated old fort, located on the east bank near the mouth of the Niagara River, was grossly overcrowded. Its commander was Colonel Mason Bolton. Besides the garrison troops (the 34th Regiment), most of the men of the Indian Department were there, as were Butler's Rangers, Joseph Brant's Volunteers, and hundreds of Loyalist refugees and their families. Winter was on its way by the time Molly and her family arrived, and they found Native refugees struggling to build crude shelters for themselves outside the walls of the fort.

For the next few months Molly was kept busy acting as liaison between her people and the British. As they had in the past, the young warriors and sachems came to her for advice. With her wise counsel and by personal example she was able to keep the Natives hopeful of better days ahead. Molly had a way of talking to them that seemed to calm their fears and defuse their anger. Because both the Indian Department and the military valued her ability to control the young warriors, they gave Molly Brant whatever she wanted in the way of materials for the task.

Daniel Claus, in a 1779 letter to General Frederick Haldimand, who had succeeded Guy Carleton as military commander of the British forces and governor of the province of Quebec (Canada) the year before, wrote, "One word from her goes farther with them [the Natives] than a thousand from any white man without exception."

Daniel Claus was back in Montreal from England, and Haldimand had appointed him as agent for the Six Nations in Quebec. As such, John Deserontyon's Fort Hunter Mohawks (in Lachine since 1777) were under his care. Claus was also in charge of the Indian Department's supply depot. Informed of this, Molly sent her old friend a list of things she needed for her stay in Niagara, particularly clothing for her children and herself.

For a long time Molly had been anxiously waiting for some word from her soldier son, Peter Warren Johnson. It had been two years since his last letter. When news finally came, it broke Molly's heart. Serving with General William Howe's British forces, Peter had been killed October 21, 1777, in a battle on Mud Island, located in the Delaware River below Philadelphia. Howe's army had taken Philadelphia that summer.

Peter was only eighteen when he died and had a promising life ahead of him. Before the war came and changed everything, Sir William and Molly had been grooming their eldest son, who like themselves was equally at home in white and Iroquois worlds. He was destined to be a leader in the Mohawk Valley.

*

By order of General Haldimand, by the summer of 1778 Molly had a house of her own in Niagara. She took a break from her political duties and travelled to Montreal, where her two eldest daughters, Elizabeth and Magdalene, were enrolled in school. The girls were surely devastated by the news of the death of their beloved older brother.

Elizabeth and Magdalene would shortly be joined at school in Montreal by the next two children, Margaret (Peggy) and George. The education of all of Molly Brant's children would be paid for by the Canadian government as Sir William had stipulated before his death.

In a letter to Daniel Claus dated June 3, 1778, Molly wrote from Niagara, thanking him for a trunk of parcels he had sent. She wrote of her concern for her brother Joseph, "who had a brush with the Rebels, but do not know at what place." The letter continued:

> "I am much obliged to you for the care and attention in sending up those very necessary articles, and should be very glad if you have any

account from New York that you would let me
know them, as well as of the health of George
and Peggy, whom I hope are agreably [*sic*] settled. My Children are all in good health, and
desire their loves to you, Mrs. Claus, Lady and
Sir John Johnson. I hope the Time is very near,
when we shall all return to our habitations on
the Mohawk River.

"I am, Dr. Sir ever
Affectionately Yours
Mary Brandt[*sic*]"

As well as the trunk of packages that reached her by way
of the Montreal trading firm Taylor and Duffin, suppliers at
Niagara, there was a gift of twenty-five pounds from General
Haldimand.

In the fall, another box of supplies came from Montreal for
Molly. This shipment included bolts of fabric to sew into warm
clothing and blankets. Molly was a skilled seamstress. There are
records from a store in Johnstown that show the sale of sewing
materials to Molly and one of her older daughters while she and
Sir William were living at Johnson Hall.

Back in June 1776, after Molly and her children had moved
to Canajoharie, Captain Joseph Bloomfield, an American officer
from New Jersey, had paid them a visit. The captain kept a journal,
and in it he wrote that on a march from Johnstown he stopped
at the home of the "well-known consort of Sir William." It seems
Captain Bloomfield had earlier placed an order for a pair of elegant leggings that were made by Miss Molly and her daughters.
Word must have gotten around about their sewing abilities.

Bloomfield also wrote about a second visit eight days later, and described Molly Brant's lifestyle: "by the generosity of her Paramour Sir William Johnson [she] has everything convenient around her and lives more in the English taste than any of her Tribe."

The second shipment from Montreal also contained a pair of gold earrings that Molly had lamented were missing from the first shipment. In a letter to Claus, Molly explained her need for "these very necessary articles" while she lived in Niagara. "The manner in which I live here is very expensive to me, being to keep in a manner open house to those Indians who have any weight in the Six Nation's Confederacy."

Mr. Taylor, one of the partners in the trading firm, assured Molly they would see that she wanted for nothing. He wrote to Haldimand, "If it were not for the service she can be of here in advising and conversing with the Indians … she would go down to Canada with the family."

In order to check on the well-being of those Mohawks who'd stayed behind in the Valley, or who had found shelter among the other tribes, Molly paid an autumn visit to some Native towns in New York State. She wanted to provide her people encouragement, and to urge them to stay loyal to the king, not to side with the Rebels nor to seek neutrality. She was back in Niagara again before the winter set in.

The constant need to maintain a positive outlook and the pressure she felt to keep the Natives onside, while grieving her own personal losses, began to be reflected in Molly's personality.

According to more than one source, she became hostile toward some of the American prisoners at Fort Niagara. Apparently, Molly told Colonel Bolton she had dreamed she'd been given the severed head of one of the captives that she especially disliked. In her dream she'd kicked that head around the fort as if it were a football.

A Mohawk woman's dreams, particularly during her "moon time" each month, were often seen as predictions, and just to be on the safe side, Colonel Bolton sent the American prisoner down to Montreal.

In order to meet what she saw as the needs of the Iroquois, Molly placed more and more demands on the fort's commander, and both he and John Butler began to lose patience with her.

Another of Molly's ongoing concerns was the whereabouts of her brother Joseph and his safety. In a letter she told the traders Taylor and Duffin that Joseph was on the frontier and thinking of working his way toward New York, but she personally felt the risk to him was too great.

According to Daniel Claus, Joseph had told Molly that he felt he couldn't do enough for the cause. She wrote, "My Bro Joseph has done; & is doing his best for the King but am only afeared he can't do enough, or as much as his Heart would fain do."

Later Molly wrote, in Mohawk, to John Deserontyon in Lachine. The Fort Hunter Natives, dependent on the Canadian government, were living there in bark huts and awaiting the day they, like Molly, could go home. On occasion, they were also taking part, under the direction of Colonel Daniel Claus, in war parties and scouting expeditions to the Mohawk Valley.

In her letter, Molly Brant told Deserontyon that a large raiding party had left Niagara on October 28, 1778, for Cherry Valley in eastern New York State. She wrote that the Native warriors were led by a Seneca chief (either Cornplanter or Sayengaraghta) but not by Joseph Brant.

The expedition to the fort and the village of Cherry Valley, to which Molly referred, was led by Captain Walter Butler and his father's Rangers. The war party also included Brant's Volunteers and a large number of Iroquois warriors, mostly Seneca. Joseph

Brant, it is said, went along with great reluctance. He had quarrelled bitterly with the arrogant Walter Butler over the way the man treated the Natives. For his part, Butler was put out at Brant's recruiting of white Loyalists, and at one point Butler even threatened to withhold food from the Loyalist Volunteers.

On November 11, 1778, while Walter Butler led the assault on the fort, the Seneca, seeking revenge for earlier losses to their own villages, began killing civilians. Unfortunately, Butler had lost control of the Native warriors after they had seen the shabby way he'd treated Brant.

Joseph Brant knew many of the inhabitants of Cherry Valley personally. All he could do to try to stop the slaughter was to take as many captives as he could, making them his personal prisoners and thereby saving their lives. Many of them would subsequently be released.

One Cherry Valley resident later reported these words of Joseph Brant. "I am Joseph Brant, but I have not the command, and I know not that I can save you, but I will do what is in my power."

Although many Patriots later referred to Brant as a "monster," it was not a fair accusation. He did what he could to save civilians in Cherry Valley. As for the raid on the Wyoming Valley in northern Pennsylvania the previous July, with its exaggerated account of civilians massacred, Joseph Brant was not even there.

*

In the spring and summer of 1779, George Washington, commander of the colonial forces in the United States, sent forty-four hundred troops under General John Sullivan and General James Clinton on a campaign to destroy Native villages in western New York State. After the Cherry Valley raid the previous November,

Washington was determined to stop the Five Nations from any further participation in the war.

The mission of the Sullivan Campaign was the total destruction of Iroquois villages. The troops were to burn the Natives' homes and their food supply, including field crops and orchards. The American troops were also under orders to take as many prisoners as possible, so that they could be used as hostages in future peace negotiations.

Eliminating the Natives' food supply would put an added strain on the British, who would be forced to provide for the Natives over the winter. The British army itself relied on the food produced in the fertile lands of the Iroquois in New York State.

*

Whether Colonel Bolton was tired of Molly Brant's demands or he was concerned with the dangerous over-crowding at Fort Niagara, the fort's commander suggested Molly and her family might be more comfortable living in Montreal. There was now the added concern of a possible attack on Niagara by General Sullivan's American forces.

In June 1779, Bolton presented the idea of Molly's relocation to General Frederick Haldimand. The governor agreed the idea was a sound one, and on July 16 Bolton wrote Haldimand, telling him that, "Miss Molly and Family have accepted your Excellency's Invitation and will leave this place tomorrow."

Although it would provide an opportunity to visit her children who were in school in Montreal, Molly later told Daniel Claus that she wasn't happy to be leaving Niagara, especially since she was leaving behind her elderly mother, Margaret, and her other Native friends. Joseph's wife Susannah had died in Niagara of tuberculosis in the fall or winter of 1778, leaving Isaac and Christina again without a mother. Equally important to Molly, the Five Nations had come to depend on her.

Claus had his own concerns regarding her coming. Would it prove more expensive for the government to look after Molly's needs if she were in Montreal? After all, she'd want to make sure that her two oldest daughters were suitably well-dressed for life in the city.

In spite of his misgivings, Daniel Claus had a comfortable house ready for Molly and family when they arrived. It was during her stay in the city that Molly told Claus everything that had happened to her since leaving Canajoharie. Her adventures were duly recorded in the man's many journals and letters.

Molly spent time with her children and was able to catch up with her stepson Sir John Johnson and to hear all his news. When John had married Polly Watts in 1773, the year before the death of Sir William, he had settled his mistress, Clarissa Putnam, and their two children in a comfortable house in Schenectady. He had provided her with an annuity of one thousand pounds and would continue to pay all her bills.

In 1778 Sir John had sent an expedition back to his home at Johnson Hall to dig up the valuables he'd buried there before he'd fled two years earlier. What they discovered was that all his papers, which he valued at twenty-thousand pounds, had been ruined and were now beyond saving, a great loss for him and for posterity.

Back in Niagara, throngs of Natives fleeing ahead of Sullivan's relentless advance were pouring into the fort. John and Walter Butler and the Rangers, along with Joseph Brant and the Iroquois, had been forced to retreat from Newtown, New York (today's Elmira), in August 1779 when they'd come face-to-face with Sullivan and his cannon. After this devastating loss, it looked as if Niagara itself was in danger of attack.

News of Sullivan's Campaign reached Molly in Montreal in early September. It was clear to her that she must return to Niagara immediately. The American forces continued to lay waste to a vast area, destroying the villages of the Cayuga and the Seneca. Where were the British while the Americans were burning Native villages and crops? After Newtown, it appeared to many as if the devastation was going unchecked. Surely the Natives would be questioning their support of the king.

Molly feared that if she stayed away her people would think she was afraid. They might even think that she knew something they didn't. She must return and assure the Natives that with their support the British would win the war and all would be restored to them in the end.

Well aware of Molly's influence with the Natives, Haldimand agreed she must leave Montreal and return to Niagara.

Haldimand wrote to Guy Johnson, "I have acquainted Col. Claus that Miss Molly is to Act as she thinks, best, whether remaining in the Province or returning to the Seneca country [Niagara], and that you and Col. Claus will give her such Presents as you may think necessary, and if she goes provide for her journey as it seems to be a Political one."

On September 13, Molly set out on the return journey to Niagara, leaving her two youngest daughters, Anne and Susanna, ages eight and ten, with Daniel Claus in order that they could attend boarding school in Montreal.

Little did Molly suspect that she would never reach her final destination.

9

Carleton Island

The first leg of the journey toward Niagara took Molly Brant and family, along with another group of Mohawks, to Carleton Island, located at the head of the St. Lawrence River, between Wolfe Island and the New York State mainland. There, high above the limestone cliffs on the southwest side of the island, construction had begun on Fort Haldimand in 1778.

Molly later described her sixteen-day voyage against the current on the St. Lawrence as "tedious and disagreeable." In some stretches of the river, rapids forced the passengers to disembark from their bateaux and to follow a footpath along the riverbank.

The group arrived on Carleton Island on September 29, 1779. Molly had been expecting to board a sailing ship there, bound for Niagara. Or, if not on Carleton Island, a little farther along in Cataraqui (present-day Kingston). No boat was waiting, however, and over the next few days none came. Colonel Alexander Fraser, the commandant of Fort Haldimand, informed Molly that all ships going to Niagara had been reserved for troops heading out to try to halt Sullivan's advance.

When Molly arrived, Carleton Island was a scene of mass confusion, with troops and supplies coming and going, and more Natives arriving every day, desperate for shelter.

The island with its twin harbours was a vital transfer point along the water route between Quebec and the forts of the interior. Supplies arriving by ship from England at Quebec every spring would travel up the St. Lawrence under the care of trained bateaux men. On the island, goods of all kinds would be loaded into storehouses until sailing vessels became available to take them on up Lake Ontario to the Niagara River and beyond.

The supplies were supposed to be sufficient to last each post for one year, and commandants were advised to try to conserve their resources. Because there was always the fear that, on one leg of the journey or another, the supplies might be lost in an accident or seized by the Rebels, each officer was urged to try to make his post as self-sufficient as possible, by growing their own crops and by hunting and fishing.

While Molly and her five children waited, room was found for them in the military barracks on the island. Having to share space with the soldiers and any family members they'd brought with them would have been less than ideal. It would be some consolation to Molly to know it was to be a temporary arrangement, only until she could carry on to Niagara.

On October 5, 1779, Molly sent a letter to Daniel Claus to explain what had happened to her. In the letter she wrote that she was afraid they might be stuck on Carleton Island for the entire winter.

She had also written Colonel Bolton in Niagara and to Joseph as well, asking their advice as to what she should do about the situation she found herself in.

Guy Johnson had told her she should wait for orders from Haldimand, and as was her custom, Molly was prepared to make herself useful in any way she could.

One of the things Molly had mentioned in her letter to Daniel Claus was her concern over the Natives' dissatisfaction with Guy Johnson's bad temper, adding that she hoped for the sake of the man himself that she would soon see some improvement in Johnson's attitude.

Guy Johnson, who had been Superintendent of Indian Affairs for the Northern Colonies since the death of Sir William, had gone to England in 1775 with the party that had included Daniel Claus and Joseph Brant, leaving his deputy, John Butler, in charge. But when Johnson returned to the American continent in the summer of 1776, he'd lingered in New York City and let his deputies carry on the affairs of the Indian Department. He hadn't shown up in Quebec to resume his duties again until 1779.

Johnson appears to have become frustrated with his role in the Indian Department, and shortly afterward he was replaced by Sir John Johnson, who himself had professed no interest in Indian affairs at the time of his father's death.

For his part, Guy Johnson had his own complaints about Molly Brant, and he'd made these known to Daniel Claus, just as Molly had done with hers. Johnson was especially annoyed at the way Molly had helped herself to anything she wanted from the government store while she was in Montreal. Molly Brant had certain expectations and could be quite demanding.

Lacking confidence in Molly's ability to adapt to the unexpected sojourn on Carleton Island, Johnson was convinced she would cause trouble for the government if she remained there. She'd never be satisfied with living in barracks, and that was the only accommodation the government could afford for her. She was to prove him wrong.

*

Ever since the retreat from Newtown in August 1779 by Butler's Rangers and the Iroquois, trying to stop the Sullivan Campaign, the Native chiefs had been asking the British to send support, under the leadership of Sir John Johnson, their "brother." Haldimand had been slow to act, fearing an attack on Montreal. Finally he agreed, and in a show of strength meant to encourage the Natives, he sent a troop detachment from Lachine, under Sir John. They arrived on Carleton Island just three days ahead of Molly and her entourage.

Quite possibly it was Sir John who persuaded Molly that, considering her predicament, she could be of greatest use right there on Carleton Island, by helping to control the Natives. Fleeing ahead of Sullivan's scorched-earth campaign, large numbers of her people had found shelter on the island, as they had at Niagara. Filled with resentment toward the British, who they blamed for their situation, the Natives nonetheless had to depend on them for assistance. The young warriors were eager to have their revenge on the Americans, and Molly got right to work, urging them to wait until Joseph Brant arrived on the island.

She sent word to the Six Nations clan mothers at Niagara, reminding them that since she couldn't be there, it was up to them to stress the importance of the Natives' continued loyalty to the king.

Sir John Johnson's troops and a large group of Native warriors were to sail from Carleton Island for Oswego, New York. There, they were to await a detachment of the 47th Regiment coming from Niagara, along with Joseph Brant and the Iroquois, before marching down the Genesee River and attacking Sullivan in Tioga, in the south-central part of New York, near the Pennsylvania border. But by the time the troops and Brant's Natives arrived at Oswego, it was too late in the season to go ahead with the plan.

Prevented from avenging Sullivan's destruction of their villages, the disgruntled Natives returned with Sir John's forces and spent the winter of 1779–80 on Carleton Island.

Molly's work among her people that winter won the praise of Colonel Alexander Fraser, the commandant, who wrote to Governor Haldimand, "The Indians uncommon good behaviour is in a great measure to be ascribed to Miss Molly Brant's Influence over them which is far superior to that of all their Chiefs put together."

*

Before winter forced him back to Niagara, Joseph Brant had tried unsuccessfully to keep ahead of Sullivan's troops, but by the end of September, forty Native villages had been wiped out, along with 160,000 bushels of corn.

Fort Niagara was packed with thousands of Native refugees, some of whom had arrived naked and starving. Conditions in the makeshift shelters and tents that now spread for miles along the east side of the Niagara River were beyond terrible. That bitter winter, with howling winds and snow that fell to a depth of five feet, was one of the worst on record, and it claimed many lives. Scores of deer and other animals that the forts depended on for food did not survive either.

Back on Carleton Island, Molly was able to mollify the Native chiefs by telling them that the British had had good intentions.

They had made definite plans to take action against the Rebels, even if it didn't happen. Some action was better than none. But those Natives from Canada who had returned to Carleton Island with Sir John Johnson on October 28, 1779, just one month after setting out on the aborted expedition, were more difficult to manage.

At Oswego they had refused to attack the Oneida, who they considered their own people, and thus never did go to meet Joseph Brant. Molly would have breathed a sigh of relief when most of them finally returned home to the Montreal and Cornwall area. But Alexander Fraser still needed Molly to help him keep on good terms with those who remained.

It appears that Molly reconciled herself to the fact that she would be staying on the island for a while. There wasn't much she could do about it anyway. Late in 1779 she received word that her brother Joseph had remarried, and that no doubt pleased her. His bride was Catherine Croghan, the daughter of fur trader and Indian agent George Croghan, who was of Irish descent, and a Mohawk woman. Catherine was twenty and Joseph thirty-six. Sources say that Catherine Brant was, like Molly, an independent, resourceful woman. The couple would have seven children and would remain together until Joseph's death in 1807.

Joseph Brant spent much of the summer of 1780 avenging the destruction of the Iroquois homeland by raiding white settlements on the Mohawk and Susquehanna Rivers. In August, he joined Sir John Johnson's King's Royal Regiment of New York in carrying out raids in the Mohawk Valley, where they burned two hundred homes and 150,000 bushels of wheat. The action became known to the Mohawk people as the "burnt earth" campaign.

Although the Sullivan Campaign had ended before it reached the shore of Lake Ontario and the British forts at Oswego and Niagara, coupled with the harsh winter it brought to an end the Native habitation in the Finger Lakes area, and it paved the way for white settlers who would move into the fertile region at the end of the war.

(On September 8, 1879, the one-hundredth anniversary of the Sullivan Campaign, a monument was unveiled in La Fayette Park in what is now Waterloo County, New York. The inscription on the monument reads:

> To commemorate the destruction of the Indian Village SKOI-YASE
> by Col. John Harper, under Orders of Major General John Sullivan,
> September 8, 1779.

Skoi-Yase was a Cayuga village north of Seneca Lake. On the opposite side of the monument are the poignant words, *SKOI-YASE. He-o-weh-gno-gek*, which translates to "once a home, now a memory.")

The Sullivan Campaign was a war against an entire people. Sources state that Sullivan boasted to Congress that "every Creek and River has been traced, and the whole country explored in search of Indian settlements ... not a single town left in the country of the five nations."

*

In the late spring of 1780, John Butler stopped on Carleton Island. He was on his way to Montreal, and Molly decided to seize the opportunity to go with him. She wanted to visit her children who were in school there, and it would be pleasant to spend some time with her good friends Daniel and Nancy Claus.

The trip worried Colonel Fraser, however. He feared that Molly might not return to Carleton Island but instead accompany John Butler all the way back to Niagara. He didn't want to lose her valuable assistance in handling the Natives.

Fraser wrote Haldimand to say he'd tried his best to keep Molly Brant happy there on the island, had at his own expense prepared a garden for her and done all he could to see that she was comfortable, although she was still living in military barracks.

Sometime in 1780 it appears that Molly's mother, Margaret, died in Niagara, and Molly may have had less interest in returning there after that.

Molly had her own agenda for the trip east, besides visiting friends and family. Her plan was to carry on with John Butler and go to Quebec, where she intended to talk to Governor Haldimand face-to-face. She was financially strapped and felt that her continuing work with the Natives should have earned her some monetary reward. Her children were getting older; a couple of the girls would soon be old enough to marry. She was also still responsible for clothing and feeding her servants. While she was living in Niagara she'd been able to provide presents to the Iroquois, and she wanted to be able to continue the custom with the Natives who passed through Carleton Island.

Any attempt Fraser might have made in the past in trying to get her a government pension had failed. Now she'd make her case to Haldimand herself.

Molly visited the Claus family in Montreal one day, taking along her son George, who was there attending school. To her surprise, when she told Daniel what she had in mind, he discouraged her from trying to see Haldimand personally. He convinced her to let him and Sir John Johnson speak to the governor on her behalf. Claus suggested an allowance of two hundred pounds as a suitable settlement, and some time later, Molly did receive an annual pension from the government. At one hundred pounds per year, it was the largest pension ever paid to a Native person.

Earlier, Alexander Fraser had told Haldimand that Molly might be happier on Carleton Island if "some little box of a house were built for her." Haldimand approved of the idea and instructed Colonel Fraser to go ahead and have the house built, "chusing [*sic*] a favourable Situation within a few hundred Yards of the Fort."

Molly returned to Carleton Island with two of her daughters and her son George, all of whom by that time had finished school. Daniel Claus reported to Haldimand, "The girls had done well in reading and writing English and George, aged 14 had excelled in mathematics."

The lad showed such promise that "with a little care and study he may easily require more of that Science than he will have occasion for." And since George's name does not appear with the other members of Molly's family on the "Return of Loyalists on Carleton Island," dated November 26, 1783, one might assume that he did return to school. Although it has also been suggested that George Johnson was away at the time the document was written, having joined Butler's Rangers.

Molly would make another trip to Montreal the following year to bring home from school two more of her children, likely the two youngest girls, Susanna and Anne. Brant Johnson's daughters, who were grandchildren of Sir William, were also being educated at the Montreal school.

Molly Brant didn't take her children's free education for granted. In a letter from Daniel Claus in Montreal to Major Robert Mathews, Governor Haldimand's secretary, dated July 26, 1780, he wrote, "At Molly's leaving this [Montreal] she entreated me to offer her most sincere and hearty Respects & thanks to His

Excellency for this essential part of the Education He ordered to give her children ... she seemed to be happy in her children's improved State and left with Satisfaction & contentment."

Before long, Molly and the family were able to move into their new house. Major John Ross had taken over the ailing Alexander Fraser's position as commandant on Carleton Island in November 1780. Ross treated Molly just as kindly as Fraser had, and she was reportedly happier now on the island than she had been before. It continued to be a busy stopover for both whites and Natives travelling between the St. Lawrence and Lake Ontario, and there was always plenty of activity. As usual, Molly kept a close eye on all the comings and goings and reported to Haldimand anything she heard that might be important.

Molly had occasion to meet an interesting woman, Mary Aaron, on Carleton Island. Mary was the sister of Aaron Hill, an active Loyalist Mohawk, and like his brother David, a friend of Joseph Brant's. Mary Aaron had been the mistress of Major-General Philip Schuyler, and, siding with the Rebels, had stayed behind in the Mohawk Valley. For this she became alienated from the rest of her family. She appears to have later switched sides because she sought the protection of Sir John Johnson during one of his raids on the Valley and returned with him to her Mohawk people on Carleton Island.

In her talks with Molly Brant, Mary Aaron revealed much information about the Rebels' movements, and Molly promptly turned over the details to the British authorities.

Among the people arriving on Carleton Island at the time was a group of captives transported from Niagara. They had been taken prisoner by Joseph Brant and his men in Harpersfield, Delaware County, New York, in April 1780. Two of the captives were a ten-year-old boy named William Lamb and his father.

The boy caught the eye of Molly Brant and she made the necessary arrangements to keep him. She may even have adopted him because he is listed with the members of her household in 1783. It was an Iroquois custom to replace a lost family member with a captive, and it is possible that William Lamb was adopted as a substitute for Molly's dead son Peter. Other sources suggest he was brought into the family as a personal servant for her son George, who was just two years older than the boy.

William Lamb remained with Molly's family for eleven years before he returned to Schoharie where he was able to reunite with his father.

Captain Gilbert Tice, whom Molly had known from Johnstown where he'd been an innkeeper, wrote Daniel Claus from Carleton Island in February 1780, informing him that Molly and the children were in good health and that they passed the time agreeably, even having weekly balls and other entertainments. It has been suggested that Molly's two older daughters, Elizabeth and Magdalene, then in their mid- to late-teens, were popular with the young officers at the fort.

The loyal Gilbert Tice, Joseph Brant's sole companion as he travelled through two hundred miles of enemy territory after leaving Burgoyne's camp for Niagara in the fall of 1776, also wrote, "Had the temper of the Indians remained as it was in the fall there would've been trouble from them, shut in as they were with a small band of the race that had betrayed them, as they believed. With persuasion Molly made their resentment disappear and they gave material assistance by hunting and by sending out scouts to guard against surprise."

That winter, 1780–81, had been mild enough that Major Ross reported being able to strengthen the island's fortifications, and when spring came he had the gardens enlarged. The island's inhabitants depended on the gardens to supply them with vegetables. In spite of a plague of insects in August, the gardens had yielded a good crop of potatoes, so plentiful that Ross was able to send fifty-five bushels to Niagara. The abundance of fresh food had helped keep the community on Carleton Island in good health.

The war was going badly for the British. On October 19, 1781, British general Cornwallis surrendered 7,073 men in Yorktown, Virginia, effectively ending the Revolutionary War, although it continued for a few more months on the frontier. The news was a long time reaching the army on Carleton Island. Only the month before, Haldimand had given Major Ross permission to go into the Mohawk Valley, joining a force from Niagara at Oswego. The Niagara contingent consisted of 169 Rangers under Captain Walter Butler and 109 Natives under Captain Gilbert Tice.

The force destroyed the community of Warrensbush, first founded by Admiral Peter Warren, Sir William's uncle and mentor. Next, they marched along the Mohawk River and attacked Johnstown on October 25. The Battle of Johnstown was the last major conflict of the American Revolution.

Both the Rebels and the troops from Niagara thought they had won at Johnstown. When Ross and his allies took off for home, the Americans pursued them. Walter Butler, commanding the Rangers, was shot and killed at West Canada Creek by an Oneida sniper. Walter's father, John Butler, had been a lifelong friend of Molly's and Sir William's, and when the sad news finally reached her, she would have understood only too well the man's sorrow at the grievous loss of a son.

One mild winter on the island was followed by a severe one in 1781–82. It was also marked by a serious fire that destroyed the naval artificers' barracks, as well as valuable stores above it in the rigging loft. Then came two summers when grasshoppers devastated Ross's precious crops.

The Natives on the island became more restive as news of British losses grew. Haldimand told Ross in all sincerity, "The Indians may rest assured they will never be forgotten. The king will always consider and reward them as his faithful children who have Manfully supported his and their own Rights."

At last the news reached Carleton Island of Cornwallis's surrender. Joseph Brant had taken a large war party to destroy what little was left of the Mohawk Valley when he was ordered to return to Oswego. The end of hostilities had been announced.

Right to the last, Molly continued to reassure the Natives that the king would not let them down. They heard in mid-May of a preliminary peace treaty, signed in Paris on November 30, 1782.

The terms of the treaty were an embarrassment to Haldimand. Each commander was told to keep the terms to himself, but word leaked out. It appeared that the boundary between the United States and British Canada was to run through the centre of the Great Lakes, far north of the Stanwix line. The Natives were thunderstruck.

As shocked as anyone, Molly tried to calm the warriors. They all must wait to hear if the rumours were true. Joseph Brant was on his way to meet with Governor Haldimand.

When he stopped on Carleton Island, Joseph visited Molly and both agreed that the governor should be told how outraged the Natives were over the terms of the treaty. But none was more so then Joseph himself. It would be up to Molly to keep her people on Carleton Island under control. She sent her son George to Niagara with a message for the Six Nations clan mothers, insisting they per-suade the warriors there to do nothing until they heard from Joseph.

10

Broken Promises

Joseph Brant arrived in Montreal on Friday, May 16, 1783. After conferring with Sir John Johnson and Daniel Claus, he carried on to Quebec, taking with him Captain John Deserontyon, leader of Claus's Fort Hunter Mohawks.

On May 23, John and Joseph met with Governor Haldimand. Joseph was determined to learn the whole truth behind the terms of the peace treaty. He reminded Haldimand of the repeated promises both he and Governor Carleton had made to the Iroquois. Now that the Six Nations were no longer needed to fight Britain's war, were they to be forgotten?

"We helped you conquer Canada and joined you in war against the rebels. You promised to defend us and our country."

Joseph reminded the governor how the Iroquois had been allies of Britain from the beginning, of all the land the Iroquois had ceded in 1768, and of how they'd protected the Superintendent of Indian Affairs and other Loyalists, helping them to reach Canada safely.

Deeply ashamed, Haldimand admitted that everything the man said was true. But he was at a loss over how best to reply. He was sure an official answer would be coming from London, but what to do in the meantime? The governor worried about the possibility of a Native uprising, sure that the end result could only mean more losses for the Natives. The fact that Joseph provoked Haldimand by telling him that the Natives were expecting to hear some proposals from the Americans any day now may have pushed Haldimand to take matters into his own hands.

Earlier, while they'd been talking to Sir John Johnson in Montreal, both Joseph Brant and John Deserontyon had admitted they might be willing to accept land on the Canadian side of Lake Ontario for any Natives who wanted to relocate. On May 26, 1783, without waiting for word from London and eager to appease Joseph Brant, Haldimand sent the provincial surveyor, Major Samuel Holland, to Cataraqui to look at land between there and Niagara as a possible site for the settlement of both white and Native Loyalists. At the same time, he set up the annual pension of one hundred pounds for Joseph's sister Molly and gave Joseph a testimonial, written affirmation of his appreciation of Joseph's "Services to the Royal Cause."

The plan had been for Joseph Brant to accompany the surveyor and then to continue on home to Niagara. But Joseph fell ill before he left Montreal and his departure was delayed. He and Deserontyon would catch up with Holland at Cataraqui Falls when they could.

The two men, together with some of Claus's Mohawks, later inspected the woods in the Cataraqui area and agreed to let the surveyor know their decision, after they'd had a chance to check out the entire north shore of Lake Ontario. Their final choice would be land about forty miles west of Cataraqui, on the Bay of Quinte.

Subsequently, Haldimand arranged for the purchase from the Mississauga. Joseph advised Sir John that it wasn't necessary to buy the land from the Mississauga because its real owners were the Mohawk. According to Iroquois legend, the Bay of Quinte was the ancestral home of the Peacemaker, who had been instrumental in bringing peace to the Iroquois and forming the Confederacy of the Five Nations.

While Joseph was busy inspecting the lands, Haldimand sent Sir John Johnson as Superintendent-General and Inspector-General of Indian Affairs to Niagara to try to calm the fears of the Natives there about what the terms of the peace treaty might mean for them. It was a chore Johnson dreaded, and he put it off as long as possible. How could he convince the Iroquois that the king had not betrayed them when he personally believed that he had?

On July 16, 1783, Sir John formally "took the war hatchet" from the hands of the Six Nations, and he delivered the speech that Haldimand had prepared for him beforehand. He told the assembled Natives that the new Canada/United States border did not affect the land that had been theirs since the 1768 Treaty of Fort Stanwix. That land still belonged to the Natives. The Seneca leader Sayengaraghta thanked Sir John for putting his peoples' minds at ease.

Then it was time to visit the western Natives and receive the hatchet from them. The Six Nations saw this visit as an opportunity to have a discussion with their people in the west, and they planned a meeting in Sandusky, Ohio, where they would talk about organizing a general Confederacy of Natives, a union of thirty-five nations, led by the Six Nations. It had long been Joseph Brant's dream.

Joseph and John Deserontyon had by this time returned to Niagara, leaving some of the other Mohawks to keep an eye on the progress of the survey along the Bay of Quinte and the north shore of Lake Ontario.

By August 26, everyone, including all the delegates and throngs of other Natives, was assembled in Sandusky. Joseph Brant addressed the crowd. He spoke of a firm and lasting union of all Natives, a confederacy that would take up the hatchet to help one another. Although he didn't say it, Joseph also hoped the British would take up the hatchet to help the Natives, in case of war with the Americans.

Later, back in Niagara on October 6, all the proceedings from Sandusky were officially confirmed. The Six Nations sent Major-General Philip Schuyler, the American commissioner of Indian Affairs, a speech signed by Joseph Brant. "The Six Nations and the Confederates have unanimously agreed to live in Peace and Friendship with Congress provided thier [sic] intentions be agreable [sic] and leave our possessions undisturbed." He also informed Schuyler that the Natives intended to insist upon the boundary line of 1768.

When notification arrived at the end of October of the final peace treaty between the British and the Americans, signed in Paris on September 3, 1783, there was no mention anywhere in it of the Natives. The British had given all the lands designated as belonging to them in 1768 to the Americans — land that was never theirs to give. The king had broken his promise and betrayed his Native allies.

Joseph Brant is quoted as saying, "England has sold the Indians to Congress." And the Natives had been left to settle their future themselves, as best they could.

Now that the forts along the frontier were on the American side of the border, the British were supposed to vacate them. Haldimand didn't want to upset the Natives by evacuating the forts and so he held onto them, in violation of the terms of the peace treaty. This suited British Lord Sydney, the secretary of state, who authorized keeping the forts because the Americans had not fulfilled all the terms of the treaty themselves. It would not be until Jay's Treaty of 1794, stipulating that the British evacuate by June 1, 1796, that the forts at Oswego, Niagara, Detroit, and Michilimackinac changed hands.

There was some debate over which side of the border Carleton Island, located in the middle of the channel, would end up on, and so it was decided that a new location for its fort must be found.

Haldimand sent surveyor Holland to Cataraqui to check on the condition of the old French fort there, with an eye on its possible reconstruction. When Fort Frontenac was found to be in better-than-expected shape, Haldimand ordered Major John Ross, then commandant in Oswego, to establish a military post at Cataraqui and to be its commander. Holland also reported that on the nearby heights in Cataraqui there was ample room for a town.

Ironically, back in 1778 General Haldimand had preferred Cataraqui as the site for a naval base for the eastern end of Lake Ontario. His chief engineer had been the one who had suggested Carleton Island as more ideal. It would be easier to defend, he reasoned, and had the advantage of two harbours. As well, the abundance of trees on the island would be useful for building ships.

In October 1783, Sir John Johnson instructed Captain William Redford Crawford, of the King's Royal Regiment of New York and the Indian agent on Carleton Island, to buy land in Cataraqui from the Mississauga for the town. When the sale was finalized, the families began to leave Carleton Island.

Back in April, at the end of the war, all work to fortify Carleton Island was ordered to cease. There had been nine ships laid up in the harbour, but now they were no longer needed.

In Cataraqui, temporary barracks were constructed inside the walls of old Fort Frontenac. By government order two houses were to be built nearby immediately, one for Joseph

Brant and the other for Molly and her family. They were to be on the west side of the harbour, near the old fort, because Molly had requested that her new house be in the town.

The orders for the construction of the houses was sent in a letter from Governor Haldimand on November 1, 1783. Because of the unique "zeal, activity and Fidelity which he [Joseph] has manifested throughout the Rebellion ... a house should be built for him and another for Molly at Cataraqui." The letter continued:

> All officers who shall Command at that Post are hereby directed to Consider the said Houses entirely the Property of the said Capt. Brant and Mary Brant, and upon no Account whatever (the event of a Siege excepted) are they to be occupied or employed for the use of the Government or any other purpose, but as herein Specified, and this Order is to be handed, together with all other Standing Orders of the Post from one Commanding Officer to another.

A second letter from Haldimand, written from his headquarters in Quebec on November 13, 1783, to Major John Ross, contained instructions regarding the Brant houses in Cataraqui:

> As it is natural to suppose that Joseph Brant would wish to have a Home contiguous to His Sister, for the purpose of leaving His Family under Her protection when called abroad by War or Business, I would have a comfortable House Built for him as near as possible (but

distinct from) to Molly's — it will give them
both satisfaction, and they can be grateful without any very great Expence [*sic*], as there are so
many Workmen employed.

By November 1783 there were only thirty-seven Loyalists
left on Carleton Island, including Captain Crawford and his
family, and Molly and hers. The troops had already moved to
their new quarters in Cataraqui, and ships no longer stopped at
the twin harbours below Fort Haldimand.

In the "Return of Loyalists, Male and Female, on Carleton
Island," dated November 26, 1783, the household of Molly Brant
is listed, along with the age of each member and the number of
rations each was given from the king's store.

The list includes Mrs. Mary Brant, age forty-seven, and
Molly's six Johnson daughters, ranging in age from Elizabeth,
who was twenty, to Nancy (Anne) aged ten. Also "Wm Lamb,
13; Abraham Johnston, a negro, 45; Juba Fundy, a Negro woman,
23; Jane Fundy, a Negro woman, 20."

Molly's son George may have gone back to school in
Montreal, but little William Lamb was still part of the household, as were the family's loyal servants, numbering now three,
instead of the original four.

*

In February 1784, Joseph Brant was again on his way to confer
with Governor Haldimand. He stopped off in Cataraqui to see
how construction on his new house was coming along. He became
concerned when he saw that Molly's hadn't yet been started. Molly
and her family once again had to live in the barracks. Joseph

threatened the authorities that if the house weren't started immediately he would take his sister and her family back to Niagara.

Already, the sawmill that had been built for the town under Haldimand's orders was busy squaring logs for the new town. Because there was very little soil over the bedrock, many of the buildings had to be erected on stone footings. Haldimand had also instructed that any houses or sheds worth saving from Carleton Island be brought to Cataraqui, pulled across the ice of the frozen St. Lawrence. Already three houses had made the treacherous journey.

Part of Joseph's mission to Montreal was an errand on behalf of the Niagara Mohawks. They had changed their minds about settling on the Bay of Quinte, and now Joseph proposed a site for them along a stretch of the Grand River where it flowed into Lake Erie. It would be closer to their Seneca brothers, who had moved to Buffalo Creek, and to the western Natives in the Ohio Valley.

Haldimand agreed to this new settlement and, along with the grant of the land, he promised the Mohawk seeds and farm implements, a school and a teacher, and a church and a clergyman for their new community. John Deserontyon and his Fort Hunter Mohawks preferred to stay in their new village on the Bay of Quinte. Deserontyon was of the opinion that the Grand River settlement was too close to the Americans.

At the Bay of Quinte they would have their own school, and a church, and one half of Queen Anne's silver communion service.

The communion silver given to the Mohawks by Queen Anne after the visit of the four "kings" to her court in 1710 consisted of seven solid silver pieces: two flagons (pitchers), two chalices, two patens (plates), and one alms basin.

When the fighting broke out at the beginning of the American Revolution, the Fort Hunter Mohawks had been forced to flee to the safety of Canada, and their priest, Rev. John Stuart, had been arrested. The Natives had been afraid to take the precious communion silver with them, and, after wrapping the pieces carefully, they had buried them in the ground along with some other valuables.

Years later, four brave Mohawk warriors, led by Captain John Deserontyon, slipped back across the border and into the Mohawk Valley, where, under cover of darkness one night, they dug up the silver. In the process, one of the spades they were using struck the side of a flagon, leaving a dent in it that can still be seen today. The Natives made their way safely back to Canada with the silver.

After seven winters spent camped at Lachine, Chiefs Deserontyon, Aaron Hill, and Isaac Hill led their followers to the land on the shore of the Bay of Quinte that had been granted them by the government. There were fifteen families making the journey up the St. Lawrence, and the communion silver made the voyage in one of the canoes, wrapped in a blanket and nestled in the lap of Captain John's wife.

The first thing the families did upon their arrival on May 22, 1784, was to lay out the communion silver on an overturned canoe so that they could hold a service of thanksgiving for their safe arrival in their new home.

About 1785, the silver was split up, with the alms basin, one each of the other three pieces, and a large Bible going to the Grand River Mohawks. The remaining three pieces would stay with the Mohawks of the Bay of Quinte.

11

New Settlements in Canada

While he was in Montreal in early 1784, Joseph Brant gave Governor Haldimand a list of all the Mohawk losses in the American Revolution and asked for compensation. The losses amounted to sixteen thousand pounds in New York currency. Haldimand was able to give Joseph only fifteen hundred and referred the rest of the claims to London for payment later on.

Joseph pressed the governor for an answer to the question of whether the British would come to the aid of the Natives in the event of war with the Americans. Haldimand had no answer for him yet. His secretary, Major Robert Mathews, tried to be helpful, telling Joseph that his own understanding of the situation was that if war occurred between the Natives and the Americans, the British could only help the Natives if they were attacked inside Canada. Clearly, that didn't satisfy Joseph.

It had been Governor Haldimand's responsibility to provide food, clothing, and accommodation for the Loyalists, and to see to their eventual settlement. Although thousands had already gone to what is today the Maritime provinces, many disbanded soldiers and their families spent the winter of 1783–84 in miserable conditions in camps below Montreal.

Sir John Johnson, commander of the King's Royal Regiment of New York, once the largest Loyalist regiment in Quebec, had been responsible for the negotiations with the Mississauga for land titles, in his role as Superintendent General of Indian Affairs in British North America. In the autumn of 1783 the purchase of the land for the Mohawks on the Bay of Quinte was completed.

Captain William Crawford wrote to Sir John Johnson on October 9, 1783, regarding the purchase. "The consideration demanded by the Chiefs for the lands granted is that all families belonging to them shall be clothed, and that those who do not have fusees [guns] shall receive new ones, some powder and ball for their winter hunting, as much coarse red cloth as will make about a dozen coats and as many laced hats. This I have promised they shall receive."

On May 17, 1784, bateaux carrying Loyalists bound for Cataraqui left Quebec and headed up the St. Lawrence, while their oxen were driven along the north side of the river, through the woods. Haldimand had given each man who would be settling in Cataraqui an axe and a hoe.

Unlike the other Loyalists, Molly and Joseph Brant did not have to draw lots for their property in the new town. Molly had been assigned Farm Lot A in Kingston Township, a total of 116 acres. Because part of the lot was reserved for clergy, Molly's allotment was not the usual two hundred acres.

*

Arrested in Fort Hunter during the American Revolution for being a Loyalist, Rev. John Stuart and his family had spent much of the war on parole in Schenectady, New York.

The Americans had desecrated his chapel at Fort Hunter, turning it into a saloon and then later using it for a stable. Stuart had not been allowed to support himself by opening a school in Schenectady, as he'd hoped, but in 1781 he'd applied to be part of a prisoner exchange. As a result, an American prisoner was traded for him, and the Stuarts were able to go to Montreal. It gave Stuart great pleasure then to be able to preach occasionally to his Mohawk parishioners who'd been part of his Fort Hunter flock.

Reverend Stuart had established a school in Montreal, with the help of a government subsidy. As well, he was made chaplain of the Second Battalion of the King's Royal Regiment of New York. Sir John Johnson's regiment had originally comprised one battalion with ten companies. A second battalion was added in 1780.

Portrait of Reverend John Stuart.

Stuart, John. 1743–1821. Library and Archives Canada, MIKAN no. 2836700.

As a Loyalist refugee, Stuart had, in December 1783, petitioned for land in Cataraqui, applying to become chaplain of the troops stationed there. He also wanted to continue to serve as missionary to the Mohawk community. He and his family were part of the group of Loyalist settlers that travelled to Cataraqui in the spring of 1784 under the guidance of Michael Grass, one of the Loyalists earlier evacuated from New York City.

In June 1784, Joseph Brant, who was back in Niagara, had a visit from Rev. John Stuart. It had been nine years since they'd last seen each other, and much had happened in both of their lives.

After first visiting Captain John Deserontyon's new village on the Bay of Quinte, Reverend Stuart had continued westward, preaching at the white communities that were scattered along the north shore of Lake Ontario. He preached at the church that Joseph attended in the Loyal Confederate Valley, a few miles from Fort Niagara. Those who couldn't push their way inside for the service filled the open windows of the church to hear Stuart's message on morality and the Scriptures.

*

The State of New York wanted to finalize a peace with the Six Nations and to get a land concession from them, particularly land around Oswego and Niagara. Governor George Clinton invited representatives from the Six Nations to a council at the new blockhouse at Fort Stanwix with the representatives of New York State. The council opened on September 5, 1784. When it was over, there had been plenty of goodwill but no land concession by the Natives.

Joseph Brant had asked Governor Clinton about the status of Mohawk lands at Canajoharie, especially that of Molly's four oldest children. Governor Clinton told him that no land had ever been confiscated, and Joseph naively believed him. Over the years the Johnson children would try repeatedly to get their land back, without success. As for the Canajoharie Natives, they had "abandoned" their land; there would be no getting it back.

That council was to be followed by another in October, this time with representatives from the U.S. Congress. Joseph Brant waited around for it to take place, but the representatives were late arriving. He felt he should return to Niagara, where Catherine had just given birth to the couple's first child, but he was also pulled in the direction of Quebec. Haldimand was retiring and preparing to leave for England.

Joseph wanted to get the Mohawk land grant on the Grand River finalized and to find out about the Mohawk claim for losses before the governor left the country. Perhaps he'd even take his queries to England himself, before the onset of winter.

Hurrying back to Niagara, he packed up his wife and their new baby, Joseph Jr., along with his daughter Christina, who was about fifteen at the time, and they boarded a lake vessel for Cataraqui. There, he got the family settled into their new home. He would have been comforted by the fact that his sister Molly was nearby if Catherine needed her. It is possible that by this time Joseph's son Isaac had already married and left the family home.

In Quebec, on October 25, 1784, Haldimand signed the grant for the land he purchased for the Mohawks at the Grand River from the Mississauga. It comprised nearly one million acres, a tract six miles wide on each side of the river, from its mouth at Lake Erie all the way to its source.

Haldimand persuaded Joseph not to go to London, advising him that it would accomplish nothing. Joseph hoped that Sir John Johnson, who was in London at the time, would bring him back the answer to the burning question of military help for the Natives from the British if there was war with the Americans.

While still in Quebec, Joseph got word that his friend Aaron Hill and five other chiefs who'd gone to the conference at Fort Stanwix had been taken hostage, to be held until all American prisoners had been returned.

The council at Fort Stanwix had not gone well. The Natives had been slow to arrive, but the meeting had gone ahead anyway, with those few representatives who were there. Because of what Sir John Johnson had told them earlier, the Six Nations believed that the land in the U.S. that was theirs in 1768 still belonged to them.

The first speaker at this council, which officially opened on October 12, had been Captain Aaron Hill, representing the Mohawks.

When Arthur Lee, American commissioner for the Indians, explained the terms of the main treaty, he warned the Natives that the king had ceded all the land in question to the United States.

On October 22, 1784, although stunned by Lee's speech, the representatives for the Natives had signed the treaty. They had been expecting only to arrange a peace, but completely overruled, the young chiefs had signed away any claim the Six Nations had to the land west of Buffalo Creek and the western border of Pennsylvania.

Back home again in Cataraqui (the only time Joseph's family would spend together in their new house, close to Molly and their cousins), Joseph Brant worried about the fate of his friend Aaron Hill.

The Hill family had been friends of the Brants for years. Aaron was the brother of Isaac, David, and the late John Oteronyente, who had gone to England with Joseph back in 1775. Both of

Joseph Brant's two oldest children, Isaac and Christina, would marry members of the Hill family.

Fortunately, the hostages were soon released, and Aaron Hill wrote to Niagara to say that the Natives should not think too harshly about what had happened at Fort Stanwix. They'd felt pressured to sign the treaty by the overbearing Americans.

Later, the Six Nations in council at Buffalo refused to ratify the treaty and denied the right of those few delegates to give away such huge tracts of land. They resolved to insist the Americans return the deeds. The Americans refused.

Now all Joseph could hope for was a grand conference with the Americans and all the Natives. In the meantime, would Sir John Johnson bring him the answer about British aid that he was waiting for?

12

John Stuart's Cataraqui

The many papers and letters of Rev. John Stuart, who had arrived in Cataraqui with his family about the same time as Molly Brant had arrived with hers, provide a picture of the growing town and a chronology of a settler's life as he made a home in the new community.

As Stuart ministered to the soldiers of the garrison and the local citizens, he detailed in his letters his relationship with the Mohawk people and discussed the difficulties he encountered in travelling between his far-flung missions.

In a report Rev. John Stuart wrote to the Society for the Propagation of the Gospel (SPG) on October 1, 1785, he remarked on the place where he and his family were now settled. "[It is] really beautiful; and as there are at present as many Loyalists at Cataraqui as will occupy the Coast as far as the Indian boundaries it will soon become a place of consequence."

When Stuart arrived in Cataraqui, after having left Montreal in July, he found no church building in the town. The commanding officer had allowed him to use a large room in the garrison as a place of worship. Now, he was pleased to report that the local inhabitants were turning out regularly for the services he held every Sunday, and he was hopeful that the congregation would continue to grow.

Stuart reported that he had already visited the Mohawks on the Bay of Quinte, his former parishioners from Fort Hunter. He really didn't want to complain, he wrote, but unless his income was increased it was going to be next to impossible to support his family in the new location. Even if the future of the area looked bright, he was finding things very expensive. "Wheat is sold at half a guinea a bushel, and other things in proportion."

The second battalion of the King's Royal Regiment of New York, known as the "Royal Yorkers," had been busy prior to the influx of Loyalists to the area. They had been given the responsibility of establishing a base in Cataraqui.

Stuart wrote that the soldiers "thought they should've been released from the army but by the winter of 1783–84 they'd built a wharf in Navy Bay, a sawmill, gristmill, two houses for the Brants, a naval store, and a considerable quantity of timber had been cut and squared for building."

Contrary to Stuart's report, the builders had not finished the second Brant house that winter. It was February when Joseph Brant arrived to find Molly and her daughters living in the barracks, and he had issued his ultimatum.

In Cataraqui, five townships were planned for the Loyalists. Although at first they were known only by number, they later became Kingstown, Ernestown, Fredericksburg, Adolphustown, and Marysburg.

*

In the opinion of General George Washington, the evacuation of Loyalists from New York City at the end of the American Revolution was going much too slowly. General Guy Carleton was in charge of the removal of thousands of Loyalists who were boarding British ships at New York Harbour and heading for Nova Scotia. It was only when the last of the families coming out of the interior managed to reach the harbour on November 25, 1783, that Carleton gave the city back to the Americans.

Captain Michael Grass had made a special request of Carleton to transport a group of Loyalist refugees to Cataraqui. Grass had spent time as a prisoner at Fort Frontenac during the French and Indian War, and he remembered thinking how desirable that area would be for future settlement.

Carleton complied, and Grass's company of 106 men, women, and children joined all the others gathered at New York Harbour. Grass's company travelled up the St. Lawrence, escorted by a British naval ship. They spent the winter of 1783–84 in Sorel, below Montreal, living in huts and tents. Sorel had become the clearinghouse for thousands of Loyalist refugees.

In the spring, together with the disbanded Loyalist soldiers and their families who'd also wintered at Sorel, they journeyed in convoys of bateaux up the river to Cataraqui.

Captain Michael Grass was given the first pick from among the lots to be drawn; Rev. John Stuart had the second. His was Lot Number Twenty-four.

Writing to his bishop, Dr. White, in Philadelphia on November 2, 1785, John Stuart said he'd been busy since his arrival, building, plowing, sowing, etc. on his two hundred acres, which were located within a half-mile of the garrison.

The town was growing quickly, and more than fifty houses had already been built, some of which he found "quite elegant."

Cataraqui was by that time, due to its good, deep harbour, the Port of Transport from Canada to Niagara. According to Stuart, it should shortly be a "Place of considerable Trade, and consequently an eligible Situation."

By this time Reverend Stuart had fourteen hundred acres in different locations, including three farms that he was improving. "We are a poor, happy People, and industrious beyond Example." The biggest disappointment to him was the lack of a school for his two sons, George and James. Still, he was hopeful that the government would approve his application for assistance in building one. This, he wrote, would cause him to live and die there, contented.

"Our gracious King gives us Land grants, and furnishes Provision &c Clothing, farming utensils &c until next September, after which, this Generality of the People will be able to live without his Bounty."

Apparently, the government did provide funds to build the school Stuart had been campaigning for. It became the first school in Upper Canada. In a letter to Bishop White in August 1786, less than a year later, he wrote that he'd opened his school in May, with thirty pupils in attendance. It was a school for boys only, however, and Molly Brant's youngest daughters would not have benefitted from its presence in the town. Having no schoolmaster, Reverend Stuart taught the students himself, without pay, for fourteen months.

"Everyone here is busied in procuring the necessaries of Life," Stuart wrote, "in cultivating Land, building Houses &c and indeed, never was the Farmer's labour more amply repaid than in the Crop we have had this season." The Stuarts' house was finished and they were ready to move in. He, and possibly Mrs. Stuart, planned a visit to Philadelphia the following spring.

When Stuart returned to Cataraqui after his visit with the bishop in Philadelphia, he wrote again in August 1787 to say that commissioners had been sent by Lord Dorchester (Governor Carleton, who had replaced Governor Haldimand) to hear complaints and grievances. Once they'd made their report it was expected that "a liberal system of Laws and Government should immediately be established among them — this will be the Capital of the new Settlement and must become a Place of Importance."

Reverend Stuart was receiving a small salary of fifty pounds a year from the SPG when he wrote to his new bishop, Dr. Charles Inglis, in 1788. In 1787, Inglis had been appointed the first Colonial Bishop. His Nova Scotia diocese included Quebec, New Brunswick, and Newfoundland.

In the letter, Stuart gave this new bishop a historical account of what had happened to him since his arrival in Canada, "so that you may more perfectly understand me." He explained that when the Revolutionary War had ended, the SPG had offered him a choice of settlements. Complying with Haldimand's orders and duty bound to follow the regiment to which he had been chaplain, he had decided he could be most useful in Cataraqui. By all accounts, he was happy there.

*

Once Molly Brant had settled into her new home in Cataraqui, one would think there would be fewer demands on her. She'd earned the respect of those around her, and she was well-treated wherever she went. Her children were getting older, and she had the choice now of sitting back and watching their lives unfold.

But Molly was in the habit of keeping an eye on whatever was happening all around her. Because of this she may well have been the first to know when a neighbour needed help, and with her knowledge of Native medicines and the healing qualities of certain plants and herbs, she may often have been called upon to attend to the sick in the community.

Sometime shortly after the family left Carleton Island, Molly's eldest daughter, Elizabeth, reportedly a popular dance partner at the various balls she'd attended in both Niagara and Carleton Island, married Dr. Robert Kerr, a physician and a magistrate.

Born in Scotland, Robert Kerr had served under General Burgoyne in 1777. Serving as a surgeon's mate, he'd been taken prisoner at Saratoga when Burgoyne surrendered to the American general Horatio Gates. After the war, Kerr had returned to Quebec, where he was a surgeon in the General Hospital. Later he was stationed at Carleton Island with the second battalion of the Royal Yorkers. When his regiment was disbanded he joined the Indian Department in Niagara as a surgeon, and it was in Niagara that he and Elizabeth would reside now that they were married.

Molly's new house in Cataraqui was spacious and comfortable. It was most likely built of squared logs and similar to that of her brother, which was forty by thirty feet and one and a half storeys. Looking south from her house, located above the gently sloping riverbank in the shelter of a bay, Molly had a pleasant view of the mouth of the Cataraqui River, the burgeoning town, and, in the distance, Lake Ontario where it flowed into the St. Lawrence.

13

A Change of Heart

Joseph Brant was building himself a log house at the Mohawk settlement on the Grand River. The town, on the east side of the Grand, would soon become known as Brant's Town, and the ford that provided a means of crossing the river on Joseph's farm became Brant's Ford. The Mohawk had their own name for the settlement: Ohsweken.

There were clearings to be cut on the almost one-million-acre tract, and land to be worked in order to get the crops planted. Joseph knew his wife, Catherine, would be happy to get back to a more traditional style of living. Sometime in the summer of 1785 he moved his family from the town of Cataraqui into their new home in the wilderness. Never again were they to live in the big house next to Molly's. When the new house was completed it would be a grand one, like the house of a wealthy white man, with two storeys and a white picket fence.

The Brants would have seven children over the ensuing years. Joseph's two older children, born to his first wife, Peggie, also came to live in the settlement. Christina, married to Aaron Hill, the son of Joseph's good friend David, had several children. Aaron Hill Jr. was an educated man and active in the church. He provided a good living for his family. Joseph's eldest son, Isaac Brant, was married to Mary Hill, and they too had a family.

Joseph Brant was still waiting to hear what Sir John Johnson had to say about British military aid to the Natives in the west. Because of continuing encroachment by white settlers beyond the Ohio River, war between the Natives and the Americans was looking more and more likely every day. Had Sir John been able to clear up the question of whether or not the British would support them?

Johnson was due back from England before winter set in. Hoping to meet him as soon as he arrived in Quebec, Joseph Brant, David Hill, the Seneca chief Sayengaraghta, and a chief from the Cayuga nation journeyed to Sir John's home near Montreal. To their great disappointment, Sir John had no more to tell them than what they already knew.

Against the advice of everyone, Joseph decided to go to England himself, sailing in November 1785 on the last ocean crossing of the year. Once in England, he went immediately to London where he found lodging with his old friend Daniel Claus and his family.

When Joseph met with the secretary of state, Lord Sydney, to explain his mission, he brought up the question of the compensation for Mohawk losses first. Because Haldimand had already filed the papers relating to this matter, Joseph knew it could be handled quickly. Then he got down to the more important business: Will the Natives, "His Majesty's faithfull [*sic*] allies," have the support of the British in case of war with the Americans?

Joseph fully expected to have a long wait before he got an answer, and in the meantime, in the company of Daniel Claus and Claus's son, William, he set out to enjoy the sights and entertainments of London.

Joseph Brant dined with the Prince of Wales, and he met often with General Haldimand, now Sir Frederick Haldimand. He had his portrait painted by a friend of Haldimand's, the Swiss painter John Francis Rigaud, and later by American artist, Gilbert Stuart. One of Joseph Brant's daughters later said that the Stuart portrait of her father, at the age of forty-three, was the best likeness of him that she'd ever seen.

During Joseph Brant's stay in London, he and Daniel Claus finished translating a new edition of the Mohawk Prayer Book, a project Rev. John Stuart and Joseph had begun before the war. When it was finished, the SPG would see that it was printed.

Finally, growing impatient for an answer to his question and hoping to be able to return home as soon as shipping began again in the spring, Joseph went to see Haldimand on March 24, 1786. Haldimand handed him over to Sir Guy Carleton. Carleton was about to go to Canada himself, as governor for the second time.

The end result of all this coming and going was that Joseph got compensation for losses suffered during the war for himself and Molly right away. Joseph's claims were for 1,112 pounds; Molly's were over 1,206 pounds. The Mohawk people, in desperate need of compensation, were awarded what they'd asked for — sixteen thousand pounds — and they were to continue to receive their regular presents. Everything would be dispensed by Sir John Johnson as soon as it could be put together and sent to Canada.

It was now time to go home. When Joseph said goodbye to Daniel Claus and Guy Johnson, whom he'd also met while in

London, it would be the last time he'd ever see them. Neither man was well, and Johnson was unable to walk without assistance.

Before he left, Joseph Brant made arrangements for Daniel Claus to send ornaments for the new church in Grand River, and he placed an order for a bell for its steeple. Although he asked for a silver communion service like the one given to the Chapel of the Mohawks at Fort Hunter, he would later be satisfied with half of the original set.

(In one of his many letters to his bishop, Rev. John Stuart of Cataraqui described a visit to the Grand River settlement during which he delivered the pieces of the Queen Anne's communion service himself.

> On the 27th of May last, I embarked with Capt. Brant & 4 other Mohawks, in an open Battoe [*sic*] and coasted along the north side of Lake Ontario, until we reached its head (about 200 miles) and from thence proceeded by Land 25 miles to the village. We were ten Days on the Voyage. At my Arrival I was welcomed by my old Friends, in the most affectionate manner; and was pleased with the appearance of their Village, which is situated in the most Delightful spot, & in the fruitfulest [*sic*] soil I ever beheld. They have an handsome Church, with a Steeple & Bell, finished within, having a decent Pulpit, Reading Desk & Communion Table, with convenient Pews. On the Sunday after my arrival, (having carried with me the Platen and Ornaments formerly belonging to Fort Hunter I preached to a crowded Audience....)

Joseph Brant by Gilbert Charles Stuart, 1786. Photo courtesy of the Brant Historical Society.

This portrait of the forty-three-year-old Joseph Brant was a favourite of one of his daughters.

The long-awaited answer about British military aid reached Joseph Brant before his ship sailed for Canada. Choosing his words carefully, Lord Sydney wrote that the Natives should conduct themselves with moderation and with "a peaceable demeanor," so that they would experience many essential benefits. In other words, "stay calm," and the king would continue to look after their future welfare.

Bitterly disappointed, Joseph knew that in a roundabout way Sydney was saying that the Natives would get no help from the British if they waged war on the Americans.

*

In 1785, while her brother was in England, Molly Brant travelled back to Schenectady to sign some legal documents. She was accompanied by three members of her family. The United States Land Commission had written her to say that they required her signature in order to transfer land that was registered in her name to the U.S. government. They seemed to hint that the American government was prepared to make her a generous offer if she agreed to sign. Her children, Elizabeth and George, were also required to establish the right to lands they'd inherited that were adjacent to Molly's.

Molly and George travelled first to Niagara, and from there, together with Elizabeth and Dr. Kerr, they sailed to Oswego. The rest of the trip to the upper Mohawk River was by bateau and on foot across the portage.

Sir William's former friend, Major-General Philip Schuyler, the American commissioner of Indian Affairs, met the family when they arrived. Schuyler told Molly that her lands had been forfeited because of her actions during the American Revolution. But because Molly's children had been minors during the war, their land had not been confiscated. If Molly and her family would come back to live in the United States, she'd be paid for the loss of her property.

The Americans were expecting something from her in return. She would take up her role as a diplomat again, in order to influence the Native tribes in the Ohio Valley who were causing so much trouble. Molly was well aware that white settlers moving onto Native land was at the root of the problem in the west, and she felt the Natives were justified.

On the journey to Schenectady she'd seen for herself the havoc wreaked on her beloved Mohawk Valley and on her former residences. It made her angry and sick at heart. Sources tell us Molly turned down the American offer "with the utmost contempt." She saw the whole thing as a bribe. Never again, she vowed, would she set foot in the United States of America. How could these Rebels who had forced her from her homeland now expect her to betray her own people and the Loyalists?

Within a year the family would learn that their lands were being sold. We know today that no part of those lands was ever returned to Molly's children.

*

Lord Stanley's reply to the question of British military aid to the Natives in the west had been negative. After learning that, it seems only natural that Joseph Brant would question his steadfast loyalty to the king during and after the American Revolution.

He had always trusted Sir William Johnson, but had the man really had the Natives' best interest at heart? If the Mohawks had stayed neutral in the conflict, might they still have their homeland in the Mohawk Valley? The Oneida had theirs. With his increasing bitterness toward the British, Joseph Brant began to contemplate peace with the Americans.

Upon his arrival back in Niagara from London in 1786, people began to notice a change in Joseph. His friend Major Robert Mathews reported to Haldimand, to whom he was secretary, that Joseph Brant had even called Lord Sydney "a stupid Blockhead."

Maybe Sir John Johnson should be the one to go to Niagara to deliver Lord Sydney's message to the Natives. He'd know how to put the best spin on it. But although it appears that Sir John had agreed to this arrangement, he never did go.

*

Joseph Brant would spend the next ten years visiting the Natives in the Ohio Valley and trying to strengthen the Western Indian Confederacy that had been his dream and that had been formed at Sandusky in 1783.

There was work to be done at home, too, on the Grand River, where he continued to try to increase the size of the settlement. He still felt responsible in some way for the Mohawks on the Bay of Quinte and the other people of the Six Nations who had stayed behind in the United States.

The American congress no longer stood by the old idea that they owned the Native lands, just because they'd won the war and signed a peace treaty with the British. Now, it seems, they were prepared to pay for those lands. If the Natives would agree to sell.

In July 1788, Joseph Brant and the Six Nations from both sides of the border met in a council at Buffalo Creek with representatives from Massachusetts. The council resulted in the sale of two and a half million acres of land that had belonged to the Seneca. From there, Joseph and the Six Nations delegates set out for another council, this one with western Natives and Governor St. Clair. Major General Arthur St. Clair was the governor of the new Northwest territory.

Some of the Natives attending the council were in favour of giving up part of their country in order to live in peace. Other tribes, the Shawnee, Miami, and Kickapoo, were willing to go to war. They didn't think they'd bother attending the council at the falls on the Muskingum River with Governor St. Clair to which they'd been invited.

Many of the Natives were late arriving at the council. In the meantime, St. Clair had had a council house built at the falls, especially for the upcoming treaty discussion.

Then, without warning, one day in early July 1788, a war party attacked the soldiers who were guarding the council house, killing one man and wounding others. St. Clair sent immediate word that the meeting would now be held at Fort Harmar, not at the falls.

While St. Clair waited for the arrival of all the tribes, rumours swirled. One in particular was most disturbing to the American authorities: Joseph Brant, although he spoke of peace, really favoured war. This was totally untrue.

In truth, Joseph was smart enough to see what the future held for the Natives, and he urged them to give up part of their land so that they might save the rest. In his opinion, the Natives should relinquish everything east of the Muskingum River. The more militant Natives in the west insisted the Ohio River must remain the boundary between them and the white settlers. For them, there would be no compromise, and they refused to go to Fort Harmar. Besides, they suspected that St. Clair had chosen that as the place for the council because of the protection the American fort provided him.

Joseph Brant and his Mohawks had every intention of meeting with St. Clair, but first Joseph wrote to protest the change of venue, suggesting instead the falls on the Muskingum as a more acceptable site for the Natives.

St. Clair disagreed. Then Joseph sent St. Clair a speech outlining a compromise the Six Nations and the western Natives had decided on in council. It declared any peace treaties that had been signed earlier by only a few unauthorized Natives invalid, and they offered to open up the question of boundaries again. They would consent to the Muskingum River as the new dividing line, giving the Americans the land east of the Muskingum, free of charge. But that was to be the end of it; there would be no more land, either given or sold.

Once again, St. Clair declared no compromise. Joseph's reply was that he would not negotiate anything else until he had consulted with the Confederacy. Then Joseph and his Mohawks turned homeward.

On the way, they encountered some Natives making their way down to the council. These they told to go home too. Before leaving the falls at the Muskingum, Joseph Brant had advised the Shawnee not to provoke the Americans. He also suggested that the time had come for them to make their own decisions, not always to seek the advice of the Six Nations. Joseph Brant had changed indeed.

Two hundred Natives did eventually show up at Fort Harmar, the headquarters of the major garrison in Ohio country. St. Clair had been instructed to pay for Native land, but he informed the Natives that the United States would not give back any land they had obtained by two earlier treaties. Some Natives continued to beg that the Ohio boundary stand.

On January 9, 1789, the Treaty of Fort Harmar was signed, and the Natives received payment for the lands they'd earlier given up — three thousand pounds to the Six Nations, six thousand to the rest of the tribes.

In a report to the American secretary of war, Henry Knox, St. Clair said the Western Indian Confederacy had now been broken, and Joseph Brant had lost his influence over them.

Throughout 1789 the Shawnee and Miami continued their scattered attacks on white settlements. Possibly seeking Joseph

Brant's approval, they showed up in Buffalo Creek in the fall of that year for a council. Joseph and his Mohawks met them on September 7. Once again, Joseph told them it would be best for everyone if they would come to some sort of reasonable agreement with the Americans.

14

From Cataraqui to Kingston

In a letter to his bishop in 1788, Rev. John Stuart reported on his missionary visits to the Mohawk settlements.

> The Society [SPG] has hitherto thought proper to call me missionary to the Mohawk Indians; one division of which, under the Direction of Capn. John [Deserontyon], your old Friend, is settled at the Bay of Quinte, 40 miles higher than this Place; and the other Part, much the largest, is on the Grand River, above Niagara, and under the Auspices of Capn. Brant, distant from hence, about 220 miles — the number of Souls under the former, is 104; and the latter 399…. I have as often as possible attended the Mohawks at the Bay, which is generally four Times in a year: — they have had some of the

materials for a church prepared some years ago;
but have not yet erected it.

Following a visit to the Mohawk village on the Grand River,
where he had spent five days, Stuart wrote about his return. "The
Mohawks landed me safe at Niagara, distant about 80 or 90 miles,
and finding no vessel would sail shortly for Cataraqui, I circu-
lated Notice throughout the settlement on the opposite shore
that I would preach there on Sunday, and give the Inhabitants an
Opportunity to have their children Baptized."

Reverend Stuart made good use of his time while he waited
for a sailing ship to take him home. Before he left Niagara,
Colonel John Butler, the commanding officer of the garrison,
along with some of Stuart's former Fort Hunter parishioners,
asked him to apply to his bishop and the SPG for permission to
move to their settlement. If he were to be placed there he would
be more convenient to the Mohawks.

As further enticement, Stuart had only to mention the terms
on which he'd consent to move, and Colonel Butler promised to
make him deputy chaplain to the garrison. Butler's Rangers and
their families had also settled on the west side of the Niagara
River, on land granted to them as Loyalists.

Obviously, Stuart did not move to Niagara. He'd already
accepted his position at Cataraqui. But it must have pleased
him to be in such demand. "The little gentleman," as he was
facetiously known (he was six foot four in his stocking feet),
was the first resident Anglican clergyman to hold services in
Upper Canada.

*

In 1787, Molly Brant's daughter Elizabeth Kerr came from Niagara and travelled with her mother to Montreal to pay a visit to Sir John Johnson and his family. It is quite possible that Molly's two youngest, Anne and Susanna, had been back in school in Montreal, and this may have been the time that Molly brought them home.

No doubt Molly discussed with Sir John the unstable situation in the west, where the American government appeared to be blind to continued encroachment by frontiersmen onto Native territory.

Within that same year, Elizabeth gave birth to her first child, William Johnson Kerr, a name that must have made the first-time grandmother very proud. Elizabeth and Dr. Robert Kerr would have a total of five children over the next seven years.

In 1787, the government assistance provided to the Loyalists for a period of three years came to an end. Unfortunately, the end of the program coincided with what became known as The Hungry Year. As a result of a serious drought the previous summer, the crops failed, and when winter came it was long and hard. Snow began to fall early and lasted until the following spring, sometimes reaching depths of four or five feet. The next year there wasn't one month in twelve that was without frost.

Forest fires killed many of the deer that the settlers depended upon for food, and those animals that survived the fires were further decimated by starving wolves. In the towns, the settlers had the distinct advantage of having neighbours with whom they could share what little they had. One story tells of a single soup bone being passed from one house to the next until all nourishment was gone from it.

People ate the seed potatoes they'd stored for the following year's planting. They made tea from hemlock and sassafras, and any weed that was edible became part of the diet. Some poor souls even resorted to eating their horse or the family dog.

In his *Reminiscences,* Captain James Dittrick (1785–1863), a child at the time of The Hungry Year, wrote:

> The most trying period of our lives was the year 1788, called the year of the scarcity — everything at that period seemed to conspire against the hardy and industrious settlers. All the crops failed, as the earth had temporarily ceased to yield its increase, either for Man or Beast — for several days we were without food, except the various roots that we procured and boiled down to nourish us. We noticed what roots the pigs eat, and by that means avoided any thing that had any poisonous qualities.

*

In May 1788, in a move to replace military government in Cataraqui with civil government, Lord Dorchester, the former Sir Guy Carleton, declared that the settlements west of the French limits above Montreal were to be divided into four districts. One of the four, the civil district of Mecklenburg, extended from the Gananoque River west to the mouth of the Trent River and included the town of Cataraqui.

In each district a Court of Quarter Sessions was established, and these went into operation in 1789. One of the judges named in Mecklenburg was Richard Cartwright, a prominent Cataraqui businessman.

A staunch Loyalist, Cartwright had been born in Albany, New York, in 1759. He'd been expelled from New York in October 1777, and until 1780 had served as secretary for John Butler's Rangers, based in Niagara. Later, as a merchant involved in the provisioning trade, he spent ten years in partnership with the wealthy shipping agent Robert Hamilton, the founder of Queenston, Ontario. The two were middlemen between the merchants of Montreal and the farmers and fur traders.

Richard Cartwright had been granted land on the peninsula across from the town of Cataraqui, and because there was no bridge between the two, he began to operate a ferry service.

In 1789, a naval dockyard was established on the peninsula, at Haldimand Cove, near Point Frederick. Cartwright gave up the operation of his ferry and, once the dockyard was established, the workmen went across from Cataraqui on a large scow. The scow ran on a cable and required five men to operate. Any civilians wanting to cross paid two pence each way, and travelled in one of two rowboats.

An astute businessman, Richard Cartwright would go on to build up the largest retail outlet in Cataraqui (Kingston). Early on he'd also realized the profitability of buying up any lots the Loyalists, some of whom were discouraged with the location of the lots they'd drawn, were willing to sell. At the time of his death in 1815, Cartwright owned 27,552 acres.

*

The new decade dawned full of promise for the town of Cataraqui, by this time known as Kingston, not the least of which was the planned construction of a new Anglican church. Rev. John Stuart had written his bishop to say that his congregation had increased to the extent that the room they were using in the garrison could scarcely hold all the people who attended his services.

He'd been grateful for the use of the room above the barracks, but it had no proper ornaments, no pulpit or surplice, no communion table. "We have been obliged to use a common table." He did have a temporary reading desk, a quarto Bible, and a prayer book that had belonged to the Mohawk Chapel at Fort Hunter. There was, of course, no bell, and "the commanding officers … hitherto allowed the Drum to beat as a Signal [to worship].

"We have collected now eighty Pounds of our Subscription for building a Church, and should have applied it before this Time, had not the Report of a new Government & Governor put a stop to our Design. For we flatter ourselves that this will be the Seat of Government, and, if so, we hope that the Settlement of so many great People here will enable us to enlarge our Plan."

A new act had been passed by the British Parliament in 1791. The secretary of state in London, William Grenville, had devised the Constitutional Act that divided the old province of Quebec into two parts, Upper and Lower Canada. The province of Lower Canada would use French civil law and the seigneurial system of land tenure, while the province of Upper Canada would be governed by English law and have English land tenure. The government of both provinces would consist of a lower house, an elected assembly, and an appointed upper house. As well, there would be an appointed executive council to assist the governor.

Lord Dorchester, governor of the old province and now governor-in-chief over both provinces, recommended Sir John Johnson as the first lieutenant-governor of Upper Canada. Because Sir John had supervised the settlement of Loyalists on the upper St. Lawrence and the Bay of Quinte, everyone seemed to expect the post would be his.

Rumours abounded that Kingston would become the capital of Upper Canada, and as Rev. John Stuart had recognized, there was no sense designing a church too small to contain all the important people who would be coming to town.

Patrick Campbell, an army captain who was on his way to Niagara, stopped off at Cataraqui in 1791 and wrote the following description of the area. He was in the town for a few days "waiting a fair wind to proceed in one of the king's sloops to Niagara."

> [Cataraqui] is surrounded with water on 3 sides. At the foot of [Cataraqui Creek] is a fine safe anchorage, and on the shore quays and wharfs are beginning to be built. The whole point of about 2 or 3 miles broad is clay limestone, not high, but with an easy slope descending to the water … the materials for building are so easy to be had here, even on the very stance of the houses, they prefer building them all with timber. I never saw a prettier situation for an inland town than this place…. The town is in its infancy as yet, but fast increasing. It is well supplied with provisions of all kinds from the fertile country behind it.

Campbell wrote that there were two companies of foot soldiers and some artillery men at the garrison, kept for guarding the king's stores that would supply the troops at the northern forts.

He and two other soldiers took a horseback ride out into the country on a day late in November, going through a thick wood for about six miles and passing several new settlements built in the middle of the woods. They would also have passed by the bark wigwams of the Mississauga people, indigenous to the area.

"On our return, we rode about a mile up the side of the Grand Lake, — passed Parson Stewart's [*sic*] house and farm ... a fine farm of 200 acres, which lies on the side of the lake, and large tracts of it clear.

"Near this place, but a little more in view of the Great Lake, it is supposed the new governor of Upper Canada will erect his residence and fix the seat of government. If so, surely none can be more suitable; everything is inviting, and it seems by nature intended for the emporium of this new country, capable of being extended to a considerable empire."

Expecting to be named lieutenant-governor of the new province, Sir John Johnson had already named to his executive council Dr. Robert Kerr and Captain George Farley, both of whom were married to daughters of Molly Brant.

There had been more weddings in Molly's family. In 1791 her second daughter, Magdalene, married John Ferguson, a young man the family had known for some time. Before moving to Cataraqui in 1783, Ferguson had for five years been barrack-master and commissary at Carleton Island. It is likely that this was where he and Magdalene Johnson first met. Ferguson was later employed at that same job while at Cataraqui before going into business.

The date of Molly's third daughter Margaret's wedding is not known, but it appears to have been sometime before 1788, when Rev. John Stuart began keeping a church register. Margaret married army officer Captain George Farley of the 60th (Royal American) Regiment of Foot. The couple would later have four children.

Instead of the obvious favourite of the people, Sir John Johnson, John Graves Simcoe was chosen as Upper Canada's first lieutenant-governor. Simcoe had been the commander of a Loyalist unit himself, the Queen's Rangers, during the American Revolution.

Simcoe brought his own officials from England to serve on his executive. "He has brought Friends enough with him to fill all the lucrative offices in his or the Government's gift," wrote Rev. John Stuart. Simcoe also had no intention of making Kingston the capital of the new province.

Rev. John Stuart had returned home after a visit to Philadelphia when he wrote, "According to my Expectation, I found our Governor here on my Arrival, but not my friend, Sir John Johnson — He has quitted the Country in Disgust (perhaps never to return ...)."

Sure enough, stung by the rejection, Sir John left for England, taking his family with him. He would not return to Canada for four years.

Reverend Stuart continued to fundraise toward the day when his new church would be built. He was not optimistic now that Council would support his petition for funds for a new church. "I promoted a Subscription amongst ourselves," he wrote, "and set the Example, by subscribing ten Pounds towards erecting a church — The Sum of 120 Pounds is raised for that Purpose; And I am now [risking] another Application to his Lordship for Nails, Glass &c. If we are successful in this, we mean to build such a House as our Funds will permit."

Among the names of those who contributed to the building fund is that of Molly Brant. In fact, she is the only woman on the 1792 founding charter. Also on the list is her son George Johnson and her sons-in-law George Farley and John Ferguson.

15

Joseph Brant's Dilemma

General George Washington had been elected president of the United States, head of the new federal government at Philadelphia, in the first presidential election held in 1788–89. Washington did not want war with the Natives, but the beleaguered settlers in the west were begging for help.

On June 7, 1790, General Henry Knox, secretary of war, under presidential order, authorized General Josiah Harmar, commander of the U.S. Army in the Northwest territory, to take an expedition and, in a surprise attack, wipe out the warring western Natives.

The American government informed the British at Fort Detroit and other friendly Native tribes the soldiers would encounter on the way that the expedition was not against them. It was meant to destroy the Shawnee, Miami, and other tribes who had not come to negotiate at Fort Harmar in 1789 and who continued to attack white settlers.

In the engagements that followed, before both sides ran out of food, the Americans suffered the most dead and wounded.

When word of the battles in the west reached Joseph Brant at the Grand River, he wondered if the Six Nations should get involved, even though he knew the Natives had little chance of victory in the end over the huge force of the Americans. He wrote to Sir John Johnson to ask for his advice.

Sir John's reply, when it finally came, was so noncommittal that Joseph had to wonder if the man had ever received his letter.

In the meantime, the Americans decided to try a new Indian policy, one of humility and generosity, and they sent Colonel Thomas Proctor on a mission of peace. He went first to a Six Nations council at Buffalo Creek, hoping to persuade some of the local Natives to go with him on his mission into the west.

For three weeks Proctor talked with the Natives and the men of the Indian Department at Niagara. The Indian Department officials told Proctor that the western Natives might very well be hostile to the Six Nations for co-operating with the Americans. Because they believed peace must come about only through British mediation, the Indian Department seemed to discourage Proctor's plan.

Prior to this meeting, Joseph Brant had already held a council at Buffalo Creek at which he had proposed that the Six Nations send its own delegation on a peace mission to the west, and he had been the first one to offer to go along.

While Proctor talked at Buffalo Creek, the Natives knew that their own peace delegation had already left. Living where they did, the local Natives did not want war, and they hung onto their position of neutrality.

Joseph Brant and the Six Nations delegation arrived at the foot of the Maumee Rapids in Ohio where the chiefs had begun to assemble for the council. Joseph wrote Sir John Johnson to say that if the British couldn't help by providing arms, he hoped they'd assist them with provisions. As for the western chiefs, with the American army on the march toward them, they wanted only military assistance.

The chiefs themselves decided that they should send a delegation to Lord Dorchester in Quebec to ask when and how much military aid they could expect, and that Joseph Brant should be part of this delegation. They would also request that the British build them a fort at the mouth of the Maumee River (also known as the Miami River).

Joseph had been expecting the arrival of Proctor and his peace mission. He was not expecting to hear the American army was on its way. He found himself in a desperate situation, unable to withdraw without incurring the wrath of the western Natives. He began to worry about his wife, Catherine, and their family back at the Grand River. In a curious letter to Sir John, he wrote,

> I know I have often been very troublesome to you in the many requests made for my own Countrymen, and indeed intruded upon your goodness; — the only one that I have now to make regarding my wife & family, who I hope you will always befriend as you have heretofore done, and in case of an Accident happening to me, I make no doubt but you'll have the goodness to make your best endeavours to procure her a pension.

Before too long, government officials in Philadelphia heard that Joseph Brant had taken up the war hatchet against them. Colonel Andrew Gordon at Fort Niagara refused to believe it, as did the American secretary of war, Henry Knox.

The western chiefs knew there was no time to waste. Joseph Brant must be the one to appeal to Lord Dorchester. Travelling by schooner down Lake Erie, Joseph and Alexander McKee, Sir John's deputy at Fort Detroit, and the other delegates arrived at Fort Niagara. Here Gordon may have enlisted them to help allay the fears of the First Nations, who had flocked there upon hearing that Joseph Brant was going to war against the Americans.

There was already another peace delegation in Niagara, this one sent by the Americans. It included a chief of the Stockbridge Natives, a peacemaker named Captain Hendrick Aupaumut. Aupaumut tried to tell the western delegates, who were on their way to Quebec, that they should not seek peace in Canada but should go to the Americans.

Molly Brant had been visiting one of her married daughters in Niagara at the time, most likely Elizabeth, who lived there, and she came to the meeting of Joseph's delegation with the Americans.

After John Butler stepped into the fray and scolded Aupaumut for coming to Canada to do the Americans' work, Molly spoke up. She demanded to know from Aupaumut why, if he was on a peace mission, he had not brought any women along?

Who was this woman who stood shoulder-to-shoulder with the men and spoke her mind? Apparently, that was not the custom with Aupaumut's people.

Like Proctor's mission, Aupaumut's, too, was stopped from going any farther. But leaving Niagara for Kingston, where they'd transfer from lake vessel to bateaux, Joseph Brant and his delegation continued on.

In Quebec, they met four times with Lord Dorchester, Joseph reminding him again of all that the Natives had done for the British in the past. He told the governor the Muskingum line was the boundary the Natives would settle for. It was apparent to Joseph Brant now that if that boundary was not accepted this time, it was an indication that the Americans intended to take all the land there was.

Lord Dorchester was about to leave for England. He told Joseph the king would continue to protect the Natives, but that their land was not his to return. He hoped while he was gone he'd get word that the Americans and Natives had made peace. On August 18, Lord Dorchester left Canada.

Joseph Brant and his deputies stayed on in Quebec and Montreal for another month while Joseph talked to various officials in the Indian Department. No one could tell him anything new. Arriving back home in October, he was only too aware that everyone there and in the west was waiting to hear the good news he would surely be bringing them.

The attacks by young Native warriors continued throughout 1791. When so many attempts at peace had failed, the Americans began preparations for war.

Henry Knox decided to send out another army, this one commanded by General Arthur St. Clair. Punishing the warring Natives as he went along, St. Clair was also to build forts to protect the future frontier.

Since Joseph Brant seemed to have influence over the western Natives, there was some talk among government officials in the United States about getting him to Philadelphia in order to enlist his help.

When Joseph reached home in October, Captain Hendrick Aupaumut was still there, waiting for him. Maybe he and Joseph could go west and bring about peace together? But Joseph knew what the western Natives were waiting to hear from him.

In the cold rain and the hail, the Natives were gathering at the foot of the Maumee Rapids to hear the report of their deputies, aware that St. Clair was advancing toward the Miami towns. Where were Joseph Brant and the deputies?

Finally, the Shawnees, Miamis, and a few Cayugas set off without them to meet the enemy. On the way, they ran into their own deputies and heard the bitter truth: no military aid was coming from the British.

On November 4, before daylight, they circled the American camp near the present-day Ohio/Indiana border. The ensuing battle didn't last long, and in the end almost half the American army was lost.

At the Grand River, Joseph Brant heard the news that St. Clair's army had been defeated. More troubling to him, he also heard the Shawnee had made it known that they considered Joseph Brant to have deserted them.

16

The Simcoes Come to Kingston

From Kingston, Rev. John Stuart continued to make regular reports on his visits and his concerns about the Christian missions he had established from New Johnstown (Cornwall) in the east to as far west as York.

"It is really a lamentable Case that in so vast an Extent from lower Canada to Detroit, there is but three Protestant Clergymen, one of which is a Presbyterian. It certainly is an object worthy of the attention of Government, even in a political Light. For, if decent, orderly men are not soon sent, Methodists and other Enthusiasts will gain such a footing....

"I have at length procured a school-master for those [Mohawks] at the Bay of Quentie [*sic*]; but as the Society allows only fifteen pounds per annum; and the Superintendent has withdrawn eighteen pounds per annum, which the former Master had, I suppose the young man I have engaged will be obliged to give it up, when the present year expires

— out of his fifteen pounds he pays four dollars per month for Boarding."

In an August 1, 1790, letter to Charles Inglis, Bishop of Nova Scotia, Stuart wrote, "My oldest Son, is now in Schenectady, and my third (ten years old) a remarkable studious promising Boy, is reading Virgil here…. Economy is necessary, when I have eight children to support with an annual income of 150 pounds."

Money was always a problem for Reverend Stuart, but one he seems at times to have resigned himself to. "Blessed is he who expects Nothing," he wrote, "for he shall not be disappointed! [Stuart's punctuation.]

"I think it is a Hardship on me to pay two Guineas for my Passage to Niagara, & as much when I return without any Allowance for that or my other Expences [*sic*]; to say Nothing of the Loss I sustain by Absence from Home."

In the meantime, Stuart heard that another clergyman had arrived in Quebec and was on his way to Niagara. "If this Report is true I hope to be excused from visiting that Quarter so frequently as formerly…. I wrote to Col. Butler earnestly requesting that during the winter, proper Precautions might be taken to provide the necessary Accommodation for their minister."

Money problems aside, winter travel was often treacherous, with sudden storms blowing in off the lake, and unsafe ice on creeks and rivers.

Plans for the new Anglican church in Kingston were going ahead. "I have, at length, the Prospect of obtaining a Church. Our subscriptions for the erection of one, amount to 120 pounds, but the money actually collected does not exceed 80 pounds. However, we have ventured to bargain with a carpenter to build a frame church of 40 Feet by 32, twelve Feet high, to board, shingle & Glaze, floor it. It is to be finished on or before Augt. Next, the whole Expence is estimated at 200 pounds."

St. George's Church was built by Archibald Thompson. It sat within a block formed by King Street East, Clarence, Brock, and Wellington Streets in Kingston, opposite the Market Place. A small, plastered frame building that would eventually be painted blue, it had square windows, two doors, and a belfry — not over the front entrance but over the back, above the altar area.

Standing on the front steps of the church, which was still without pews inside, the new lieutenant-governor, John Graves Simcoe, and his executive council were sworn in on Sunday, July 8, 1792.

Molly Brant would undoubtedly have been part of the crowd that attended the ceremony. Reports say that her brother, "the great Chief Brant, known as Tyendinaga, who owned a house in Kingston was there." He did own a house in the town, but by this time he was using it only as a place to rest on his way from one Native council to the next.

Four of Lieutenant-Governor Simcoe's appointed councillors came with him from England, and the people's representatives in the first government included Robert Hamilton from Queenston and Kingston's Richard Cartwright.

Following the swearing-in ceremony, Simcoe and his executive council held their first meeting in the Commandant's house. The little blue house would be home to the Simcoes whenever they were in Kingston.

A week later, Simcoe's wife, Elizabeth Posthuma Gwillim, who had come to Upper Canada from England with her husband and who was an artist and diarist, wrote, "Sunday, July 15, 1792. I went twice to Church. The clergyman, Mr. Stuart, preached good sermons with an air of serious earnestness which made them very impressive."

Watercolour of Governor and Mrs. Simcoe's house in Kingston, 1792.

Besides her diaries, Elizabeth Simcoe's legacy included a large number of watercolour paintings and drawings that portrayed life in Upper Canada in the 1790s.

The Simcoes did not stay long in Kingston. Within two weeks they were on their way to Niagara. Lieutenant-Governor Simcoe made Newark (today's Niagara-on-the-Lake) the seat of government, and he spoke to the members of his elected assembly and executive council there on September 17, 1792. According to sources, Molly Brant and her daughters attended the opening of Parliament.

The Simcoes had brought their two youngest daughters with them from England. Their other four children remained behind in the care of an aunt. Elizabeth had been a wealthy heiress when she married John Graves Simcoe. Accustomed to the finer things in life, she — like Molly Brant leaving the luxury of Johnson Hall and moving to Canajoharie — brought with her to Upper Canada some of her oak and cherry furniture, and her delicate linens, china, and ornaments. Unfortunately for Mrs. Simcoe, she was to spend much of her time in Upper Canada living in a tent.

During his time in office Simcoe did much to improve the system of roads to aid in the defence of Upper Canada, building Yonge Street from Lake Ontario north to Lake Simcoe, and Dundas Street between London and York. But during his four-year term he paid little attention to the Loyalist settlements east of Kingston, being more concerned with the western part of the province.

In order to increase the population of his province, Simcoe invited Americans who were fed up with the lawlessness and corruption in the United States following the American Revolution to apply for land grants in Upper Canada.

One of Simcoe's most humanitarian acts while he was the lieutenant-governor was the Act Against Slavery. Passed on July 7, 1793, the Act would ban further importation of slaves and grant gradual emancipation to those born in the province. Simcoe had hoped to abolish slavery altogether, but, in any case, his act was the first to limit the practice of slavery in the British Empire.

Many wealthy families in Upper Canada owned black slaves, including Molly Brant's and Rev. John Stuart's. Molly's three loyal servants had accompanied her from Carleton Island when she relocated to Cataraqui. They were three of the four who'd fled with her from Canajoharie in 1777. Jenny (Jane) had been left to Molly in Sir William's will, along with one quarter of all his other slaves. Jenny's sister Juba and the man Abraham were likely two of that number.

Reverend Stuart's man was referred to as a body servant. He used to go ahead of Stuart to church on Sunday evenings where he would light the candles on the ends of the pews to illuminate the evening service.

Reverend Stuart took Simcoe's choice not to make Kingston the seat of government for Upper Canada almost as a personal affront. On March 11, 1792, he wrote Bishop Inglis:

> My private affairs oblige me to visit Philadelphia in May or June next. I have two sons in Schenectady. The eldest I shall place at Philadelphia College, under the Patronage of my old Friend Bishop White. The youngest I must bring home again, as my Finances will not enable me to maintain them both Abroad at the same Time. My three other sons are under the Tuition of a good Latin master here. My Expectations are greatly frustrated by Gov. Simcoe's Plan. Had he made this his seat of Government, I would have expected a Seminary, Academy or College at this Place, in that Case I might have been able to educate all my sons: But as Matters are now in-Circumstanced unless something is added to my Salary (which I do not expect) I must be contented manufacturing Farmers, instead of Diviners.

17

The Tyranny of Isaac Brant

Early in January of 1792, while the citizens of Kingston were preparing to meet the first lieutenant-governor of Upper Canada, Joseph Brant was thinking seriously of going to Philadelphia to talk with government officials in that capital about a peaceful solution for the troubles in the west. He'd heard that he might be asked, but he'd let it be known that he had first to receive an official invitation.

With its wording carefully vetted by President George Washington, the invitation Joseph had been waiting for came from Henry Knox, the American secretary of war. "The President of the United States will be highly grateful by receiving and conversing with a chief of such eminence as you are, on a subject so interesting and important to the human race."

Knox told Joseph the United States wanted to end the war between themselves and the western Natives because it would inevitably destroy the Natives. Neither did the U.S. want any more land, other than that already ceded to it by treaty.

Colonel Gordon, at Niagara, told Joseph that he disagreed with the visit. In his opinion, Philadelphia was not the place to negotiate peace because the western Natives would not be represented. They were already jealous enough of the Six Nations.

Upon consideration, Joseph Brant let Secretary Knox know that he *would* come, but just not right away. He had decided to seek the approval of the Natives in the west, and he sent a message about the matter to Miami country. He also wrote Alexander McKee at Fort Detroit to get his opinion.

It is doubtful that either party responded positively. Joseph Chew of the Indian Department in Montreal, speaking for Sir John Johnson, was firmly against the visit. But Joseph decided to go to Philadelphia anyway, once he had made sure that he would still be welcome in spite of the delay. The only one who encouraged Joseph to go ahead with his visit was John Butler, who was now an old man and unwell.

The agent for the American Six Nations, Israel Chapin, had been given four hundred dollars to pay for Joseph Brant's trip. Joseph was also assigned a guide who'd look after all the little details, horses, meals, and lodging along the way. The pair had another travel companion: Joseph's son Isaac went along with them as far as Canandaigua, where he was planning to buy himself a horse.

Joseph arrived in Philadelphia on June 20, and at noon the next day he met with the president. In a private letter, Washington wrote, "I have brought the celebrated Captn. Joseph Brant to this City, with a view to impress him also with the equitable intentions of this government toward *all* the Nations of his colour."

Rev. John Stuart of Kingston, a man who knew Joseph well, was of the opinion that the Americans overrated Joseph Brant's ability to influence all Native people. After what had happened at Fort Harmar, Joseph may well have agreed with him, but he kept it to himself.

Following the meeting with President Washington, Joseph Brant met several times with Knox, always urging his Muskingum River boundary, insisting that the Natives who'd sold the land at the Fort Harmar Treaty in 1789 had no right to do so. Knox was in no position to back down, knowing that land west of the Muskingum was already settled.

Knox told Joseph that if the compensation had not been enough, or if there were more claims, adjustments would be made. The Natives would receive their compensation annually. A treaty was going to be necessary in order to finalize everything.

Joseph advised Knox that his mission was only to bring the American proposal back to a Native council that would meet at the foot of the Maumee Rapids shortly. And he wasn't going to commit to anything until he had the approval of the Canadian government.

On June 28, the visit ended, and Joseph Brant set out for home with fifty guineas in his pouch. Knox had also seen to it that another four hundred dollars was made available for the return trip.

Out west in Pittsburgh, the newly appointed commander of the American army in the west, General Anthony Wayne, had been preparing for another invasion into Native territory. But after Joseph Brant's visit, Knox wrote that Wayne should not do anything to increase tension with the Natives. Knox was pinning his hopes on Joseph's ability to bring about a treaty.

Joseph arrived back home on July 24. Apparently, Sir John Johnson had heard a favourable account of the way Joseph had conducted himself in Philadelphia and he sent word of this to Niagara, through Joseph Chew.

Now, Joseph Brant had to wonder about the wisdom of attending the council at the Maumee Rapids. How would he be received? He wrote to Alexander McKee in Detroit to see what he thought. McKee sent him a letter saying he thought he should go ahead. Unfortunately by this time, Joseph, whose health lately had not been good, was ill.

McKee sent him a second letter, a more urgent one, from the Maumee River, where he had a house, and where he'd gone for the annual distribution of presents to the Natives. McKee hoped Joseph would be better soon because his presence there was of the utmost importance.

Still unwell, Joseph decided to entrust his son Isaac to deliver the American proposal, and Isaac Brant left the Grand River with six other Mohawks in mid-August.

The council that had been set for the Rapids was now moved up to the point where the Maumee and the Auglaize Rivers meet, in northwestern Ohio, a place referred to as The Glaize. From this vantage point, the Natives could keep a better eye on the movements of General "Mad" Anthony Wayne. They'd heard he'd built a new fort and was provisioning it. The Natives waited anxiously for Joseph Brant's arrival. What had he learned in Philadelphia?

They were in for a surprise. Arriving at The Glaize on September 13, Isaac Brant told the Natives he'd come to help them fight, and that his father wanted to warn them not to listen to the peace proposals Hendrick Aupaumut was bringing them. Isaac didn't bother telling them about the Americans' offer of further compensation, either.

Chief Red Jacket, who spoke for the Seneca, tried to get the Natives to understand that nothing could be gained by war. "You were very fortunate that the Great Spirit above was so kind as to assist you to throw the Americans twice on their back when they came against your villages, your women & children. Now Brothers, we know that the Americans have held out their hands to offer you peace … let us go on in the best manner we can to make peace with them."

Hendrick Aupaumut also had his say, but Isaac Brant had done his worst. The war party won. There would be no further discussion of the American proposal.

The western Natives sent a message themselves to the Americans, insisting the Ohio River would be the boundary between them. They wanted their country restored, and they did not want the Americans' money. The Americans must remove their forts north and west of the Ohio. These were the conditions under which the Natives would make peace. If the Americans agreed, the Natives would meet them the following May at Sandusky, Ohio. The British, too, were to be there. It was October 9 when the council ended.

Now well enough to travel, Joseph Brant reached The Glaize on October 11. Only a few Natives were still there, and Joseph told them what had taken place during his talks in Philadelphia. His message came too late.

When he reached the foot of the Rapids on his way home, he met some of the Natives who'd been at the council, and they invited him to meet in Sandusky in May, telling him they had insisted on the Ohio River boundary. With a heavy heart, Joseph promised he would meet them at Sundusky. By November 8, he had returned home again.

18

The Struggle for Peace

It is said that Elizabeth Simcoe, wife of the lieutenant-governor of Upper Canada, befriended Molly Brant while the Simcoes were in Kingston. The two women may well have met for the first time following a service at the Anglican church.

In 1792, John C. Ogden, an American traveller touring Upper and Lower Canada, wrote of seeing Molly Brant in church. "We saw an Indian woman, who sat in an honourable place among the English. She appeared very devout during divine service, and very attentive to the sermon. She was the relict of the late Sir William Johnston [*sic*] superintendent of Indian affairs, in the then province of New-York, and mother of several children by him who are married to Englishmen...."

Ogden was correct. Five of Molly's six daughters married well-respected white men. After Elizabeth and Dr. Robert Kerr were married in 1783, John Ferguson, whom Magdalene married, became the Kingston member of the Legislative Assembly of Upper Canada. Margaret married Captain George Farley; Susanna married Ensign Henry LeMoine; and the youngest, Anne, married Captain Hugh Earl of the Provincial Marine. Earl Street in Kingston is named in his honour. Only Mary, the fourth daughter, remained single all her life.

John C. Ogden told how, whenever Native ambassadors came to Kingston, Molly Brant would be invited to dine with them at Governor Simcoe's home. Molly was "treated with respect by himself, his lady, and family." Ogden noted that she dressed "in the habit of her country."

Since her Johnson Hall days, it seems, even when her daughters dressed in fancy gowns, Molly wore her traditional Native garments. It no longer bothered her as it used to that her daughters preferred to dress in the English style.

There had been an occasion once while the family was living in Niagara where the older girls had suffered demeaning racial comments by some British army officers. At the time, the girls all dressed in their traditional clothing.

When later that same day Molly's daughters had gone to a ball wearing satin gowns, the soldiers had recognized them and apologized for their earlier behaviour. The young women had stalked away, refusing the officers' invitations to dance.

*

In a letter to Bishop Inglis, dated August 20, 1792, Rev. John Stuart wrote that he hadn't gotten to see Lieutenant-Governor Simcoe until the man had been in Kingston eight days because Stuart had been away. "He is now at Niagara and apparently means to fix the seat of government there for two or three years."

The new Legislative Assembly would meet in Newark (today's Niagara-on the-Lake) in mid-September, and Simcoe had asked Stuart to attend as Chaplain to the Upper House. This was a great honour and, as Stuart wrote, "it will give me another opportunity of visiting the Indians on the Grand River."

He was able to report that his church in Kingston was covered, floored, and nearly "plaistered," also that the Mohawk Church on the Bay of Quinte was now finished. Some of his hopes for centres of education in Kingston were to be fulfilled after all. "The Governor proposes to erect a good Grammar School here, and another at Niagara, and he has a College in Contemplation.... "

Before he was sworn into office as lieutenant-governor, Simcoe met with Alexander McKee, captain and interpreter (he was married to a Shawnee woman) in the British Indian Department. It was the spring of 1792, and McKee had come down to Quebec from Detroit. The two men talked over the various Native treaties, particularly Sir William Johnson's 1768 Treaty of Fort Stanwix, with its boundary line that began on the Ohio River. That was the line Simcoe preferred because it fixed a Native state, a barrier nation between the United States and Canada.

The Americans were vehement about there being no British interference in their troubles with the western Natives, and Simcoe had given clear instructions to McKee that at the council at The Glaize, it must be made to look as if the Native people themselves had asked for British mediation in the war.

As Simcoe had hoped, the Natives *had* asked that the British be present in Sandusky, Ohio, where they were to meet with the Americans in May 1793 to discuss their proposal for peace. They had sent their message setting out their conditions for peace to Henry Knox, and he'd replied that the American president hoped all Native nations would be represented at the Sandusky Council. He'd also let them know that all war parties on either side were to cease.

While preparations were being made for the peace council, Simcoe heard from Philadelphia that the Americans would not allow British representatives at the meeting. Simcoe sent word to the western Natives that he could not go to Sandusky. Since he was forbidden to attend, the lieutenant-governor set out for Detroit, where he warned McKee to keep a low profile at the council.

Meanwhile, the western Natives decided to hold a private council of the Western Indian Confederacy at the Maumee Rapids, before going on to Sandusky to meet with the Americans.

Three American commissioners, chosen to negotiate peace at the Sandusky Council, arrived in Newark near the end of May 1793. Because they were in his capital, Lieutenant-Governor Simcoe felt it was his duty to invite them to stay at his home, Navy Hall, an old barracks across the river from Fort Niagara. The men were there for six weeks, waiting to hear that the western Natives had wrapped up their preliminary council at the Rapids and that everyone could now go on to Sandusky.

Simcoe's guests were still there when Newark celebrated the king's birthday on June 4. The three Americans got to take part in all the festivities, including a grand ball in the evening.

At the same time, Molly Brant and her family were also in Newark to attend the wedding of her daughter Susanna. The young women of the Johnson family, and quite possibly Molly herself, attended the king's birthday ball as members of the elite society. One of the three American commissioners, General Benjamin Lincoln, wrote later that he had seen them there. "They appeared as well dressed as the company in general and intermixed with them in a manner which evinced at once the dignity of their own merits and the good sense of others...."

No doubt there was much talk that evening about the news that Britain and France were again at war. With France an old ally of the United States, Lieutenant-Governor Simcoe was more than a little worried about a possible invasion of Upper Canada.

The next day, June 5, 1793, Susanna Johnson married Ensign Henry LeMoine of the 24th Regiment of Foot.

*

Fortunately for Joseph Brant, Simcoe had intervened to get him reconciled with the Seneca, and after a council at Buffalo Creek with the Six Nations, he was sent as a delegate to the preliminary Native council at the Maumee Rapids. Simcoe had confidence in him, after hearing how well Joseph had conducted himself in Philadelphia.

Simcoe had instructed John Butler and Alexander McKee that they were to explain the American offers to the Natives, and on no account were they to let the Americans think they were influencing the Natives.

Joseph reached the Maumee Rapids sometime around May 22. He should not have been surprised to find the western Natives still resentful about his not being with them when they defeated St. Clair. After some initial wrangling, it was decided that a delegation be sent to Newark to ask the three American commissioners if they had the authority to set a new boundary line. Joseph Brant and John Butler were to be among the delegates.

By this time, the three Americans had already left Niagara and were waiting at Fort Erie to board a boat that would take them across the lake and on to the mouth of the Detroit River.

Joseph and the other delegates met them at Fort Erie, and it was there that both sides decided they should have a conference together with Lieutenant-Governor Simcoe.

The group met on July 7, back at Newark. Speaking on behalf of the Natives, Joseph told everyone that the news that General Anthony Wayne was advancing with his troops gave the Natives no choice but to refuse to go to Sandusky.

The commissioners assured the Natives that Washington had forbidden any such hostilities, and the Americans reiterated that at Sandusky there'd be discussions on a new boundary line, although admittedly there might have to be concessions on both sides. Once Joseph promised that there would be representatives at Sandusky from all the nations that owned the land, the council ended and everyone headed off to the west again.

Simcoe hoped he could trust Joseph Brant. "I believe that He considers the Indian Interests as the first Object — that as a second, tho' very inferior one, He prefers the British, in a certain degree, to the people of the States," he wrote to Henry Dundas, the new colonial secretary.

On July 21, the three American commissioners were stopped at the mouth of the Ohio River, permitted to go no farther. Meanwhile, hundreds of Natives were waiting at the Maumee Rapids. When Joseph Brant and the delegates got back, Joseph told the Natives that the American commissioners did indeed have the authority to draw up a new boundary. But the Natives had changed their minds. Some of them were angry that Joseph Brant had been the one to speak for them in Niagara.

Then followed weeks of disagreements between the Native groups. Joseph wrote to Simcoe asking him to give the Natives some advice regarding the boundary. He was still holding out for his preferred Muskingum line, and he had some supporters.

Others wanted the Ohio River boundary. Simcoe's answer was that the Americans had asked him to stay out of it. Therefore, the Native people would have to decide on the boundary on their own.

More delegations were sent to confer with the three commissioners where they waited. But there was no unity among the Native nations. Back and forth it went with the Natives unable to agree among themselves. Tired of waiting, the American commissioners let them know that although they wanted peace, they were ready to go home. The sailing ship lay at anchor.

On August 16, the Natives delivered an uncompromising speech to the three Americans. They repudiated all previous treaties, said they didn't want any money, and suggested the American government use that money to evict the people who had settled on Native land. It was signed by representatives of sixteen nations, although undoubtedly every one of them included a number of dissenters.

The next day the commissioners boarded the schooner *Dunmore* and sailed away.

For the rest of his life Joseph Brant blamed Alexander McKee and John Graves Simcoe for the failure of the negotiations. But Simcoe had other things on his mind. He'd decided Newark was too vulnerable to an attack by the Americans and was preparing to move the province's temporary capital to Muddy York.

19

Defeat of the Western Natives

In spite of the lack of any agreement at the Maumee, Joseph Brant wrote to Lieutenant-Governor Simcoe on September 2, 1793, to say he was still hopeful that the Muskingum line could be the basis for peace with the United States.

Another Six Nations council was held at the new Central Council Fire, Buffalo Creek (today's Lewiston, New York), with Joseph putting forth his boundary as the line endorsed by the Six Nations. The Seneca wanted to see that line extended to follow the Genesee River to its mouth. Part of Joseph's proposal also included allowing the Americans to keep what land they had already settled beyond the boundary.

By late 1793, war between the U.S. and Britain was looking more and more possible. The British were stopping American ships at sea, impressing American sailors, and interfering with trade between the U.S. and France. Colonial Secretary Henry Dundas was urging Canadians not to do anything to trigger hostilities with the Americans.

Lord Dorchester, newly returned to Canada, told a delegation of western Natives, supposedly in confidence, that war between the U.S. and Britain was likely, and that if Britain and their Native allies won, the Natives could set any boundary they liked.

When that conversation reached Joseph Brant's ears, he felt most encouraged; the British aid he'd wanted for so long could be just around the corner.

The new year, 1794, brought grief to Molly Brant. In January, her beloved oldest daughter, Elizabeth, who was married to Dr. Robert Kerr, died in childbirth. She was only thirty-two. Elizabeth left five young children, including her newborn, a son named Robert Joseph Kerr. Elizabeth's husband would never remarry.

In March of that year, Rev. John Stuart wrote a letter to Rev. William Morice. He said he had visited the Mohawks on the Bay of Quinte, and that as soon as Lord Dorchester sent the glass and nails that Stuart had ordered, the school and the schoolmaster's house, built by the Mohawks themselves, would be finished.

Reporting on his church at Kingston, which was now called St. George's, "The Pulpit, Reading Desk and thirty-one Pews, with a Communion Table were finished before Christmas last. But finding the House too small for the congregation we agreed to erect six more Pews, and a Gallery for the Soldiers…." Every Sunday a parade of soldiers marched from the garrison to the church where Molly Brant had her own private pew.

The gallery Stuart mentioned, added in 1795, was in a rather unusual location, over the communion table rather than above the entrance. In 1802, the church would be enlarged by twenty feet in length and a second gallery installed.

*

Lieutenant-Governor Simcoe, in March 1794, stopped at the Grand River to see Joseph Brant. He was on his way to the Maumee, under orders from Lord Dorchester to rebuild an old fort on that river, as an outpost for the defence of Detroit. Before long, Fort Miamis was ready and garrisoned with a detachment of British soldiers.

This action ended any idea of holding another peace council between the Natives and the Americans, as had been suggested by Henry Knox. The western Natives were pleased to have the fort in their midst, and they were ready for the impending war between the Americans and themselves, allied with the British, of course.

American general Anthony Wayne continued his advance. Belying his nickname, "Mad" Anthony had planned his troop movements very carefully, determined to avoid any chance of being ambushed. Wayne was a strict disciplinarian and his volunteers were well-trained. Looking ahead to the day he would take Detroit, Wayne built Fort Defiance at The Glaize.

Meanwhile, the Natives at the Maumee and the Auglaize Rivers were getting ready for him. While they waited, they decided to attack Fort Recovery, which the Americans had built at the site of St. Clair's battle. In the ensuing siege, the Natives lost many warriors, even before the arrival of General Wayne's army.

On August 20, 1794, the Natives, who had prepared an ambush for the enemy, lay hidden in tall grass amongst a tangle of fallen and uprooted trees, in an area once devastated by a severe storm.

Wayne's army came on, with the Natives breaking their cover and firing the first shots. Earlier, a large number of them had gone to get provisions from McKee in Detroit, and now, hearing the sounds of battle, they turned back, joined by some white Loyalists from Detroit.

Driven from their hiding places, and their retreat blocked by the Americans, the Natives fled toward Fort Miamis. To their horror, when they reached the fort — the fort they thought the British had built for them — they found its doors shut. No one let them in.

The Natives continued their desperate flight down the river to Swan Creek, where the Maumee empties into Lake Erie.

The Battle of Fallen Timbers, as it became known, was all over in an hour. The Americans now had possession of the battle-field, and they burned everything in sight, including Alexander McKee's house. The Natives lost so many chiefs they could not fight again. The crisis was over.

For some time, General Wayne marched back and forth in front of the British fort, trying to antagonize its commander, Major William Campbell, into action. But Campbell managed to keep himself and his men in check. He was not going to start a war with the Americans.

Many of those western Natives who had lost their homes as a result of Wayne's army would settle at Swan Creek, in a camp under McKee's direction.

Joseph Brant, waiting for the army Simcoe was to send, had not been part of the rout of the western Natives at Fallen Timbers. It was all over by the time he got himself moving. Simcoe, apparently, had been gathering men to defend Detroit against a possible attack.

Joseph got to Detroit himself by September 16. There was no sign of Simcoe. The lieutenant-governor had decided against going to Detroit when he heard, on August 31, of the Natives' defeat.

Arriving at the camp at Swan Creek at the end of September, Joseph Brant found Simcoe already there. Together the two set out to survey the place of General Wayne's victory. What must have been going through their minds?

Joseph Brant had admitted that he was going to this war reluctantly. He had to have known, whether the western Natives had sent for him or not, how desperate the situation was. Simcoe sloughed off Wayne's victory as "a trifling advantage," for the Americans, and Joseph was still asking when the Natives could expect British military aid. He and Simcoe arrived back at Fort Erie on October 17.

Finally, news of Wayne's victory and the story of the British locking the retreating warriors out of Fort Miamis reached the ears of all the American Six Nations. They were stunned. In the west, the Natives denounced Simcoe, Brant, and the British Indian Department as traitors. Over the winter, small groups of western Natives slipped off to Wayne's camp at Fort Defiance to make their own peace with him. Joseph Brant's influence over them was no more.

Earlier that year, the American John Jay had gone to England to try to negotiate another peace treaty with the British. Having enough trouble already with France, Britain did not want trouble with the Americans. When Jay's Treaty was signed in November 1794 it provided for the British to relinquish the border forts on the American side of the border, effective in June 1796.

On August 3, 1795, the Native chiefs met with General Wayne and the Treaty of Fort Greenville was signed. With the establishment of the Greenville Treaty Line, the Natives gave up eastern and southern Ohio and part of present-day Indiana. The western Natives were put under the protection of the Americans. The Natives were fed up. The British were not going to help them, and they were tired of fighting alone.

It would have been cold comfort to Joseph Brant when Sir John Johnson finally returned to Canada in 1796, to hear him say that Joseph had been right about trying to treat with the American commissioners back in 1793. In fact, Sir John said, if

Joseph's advice had been taken, the Natives might have saved much of the land they lost.

*

Molly, too, had been in Niagara the summer of 1794. She may have been helping to care for Elizabeth's children since their mother's death, or tending to other matters of family business, but certainly she would have had the opportunity to talk to Joseph following the Battle of Fallen Timbers.

She would have shared with him her deep-seated mistrust of the Americans. Molly had little confidence that anything could be done now to save the Natives' land in Ohio country, and she felt sick at the news that the British had closed the doors of the fort on her people.

After Joseph left for Detroit, Molly felt even more depressed and just wanted to go home to Kingston on the first ship out of Niagara.

Lieutenant-Governor Simcoe was sending his family to Quebec City for a while, in case of the outbreak of war in Upper Canada. The ship, the *Mississaugan,* had been commandeered for Elizabeth Simcoe and her two children. Orders were that no other passengers were to be allowed aboard, but there was Elizabeth's friend Molly, looking for passage to Kingston.

"I relented in favour of Brant's sister who was ill and very desirous to go," Elizabeth wrote. "She speaks English well and is a civil and very sensible old woman." Compared to Mrs. Simcoe's thirty-two years, Molly, who was fifty-eight at the time, probably seemed old. And indeed, she was feeling quite unwell.

Molly was to see her English friend again. In the spring of 1795, when war seemed less likely, Simcoe went to Quebec himself and brought his family back to Upper Canada. They stopped off in Kingston, and while they were there Simcoe became ill. He was so sick that he spent a whole month confined to his bed.

Elizabeth Simcoe wrote that all there was available to them, by way of medical assistance, was a horse doctor. Then she remembered Molly Brant and her Native medicines, how she often visited the sick in town and was able to help them.

Sure enough, "Capt. Brant's sister prescribed a root [possibly calamus root] ... which really relieved his cough in a very short time."

In the Mohawk culture, before anyone can be healed both parties and the room itself must be cleansed of negative energy, bad thoughts and feelings. Before attending to John Graves Simcoe, Molly may have performed a smudging ceremony, burning dried herbs, most likely sage, and washing in the sacred smoke by brushing it over herself and Simcoe. Once cleansed of negativity, the healing could come through without obstruction.

Molly herself was suffering from painful rheumatism, and after a while she went to live with her daughter Magdalene and her husband John Ferguson, a member of the Legislative Assembly. It turned out to be a wise move. Not only were there small children in the household to add some joy to Molly's days, but she also had the pleasure of meeting the many guests that came to the Ferguson house. For a while life was almost as it used to be, for Molly was still a well-respected woman in her own right.

The Ferguson house was not without its sorrows, however. None of those youngsters whose games had so delighted their grandmother lived beyond childhood.

Then, tragic news came from the Grand River: Molly's nephew Isaac, Joseph Brant's oldest son, had died late in 1795.

Molly was reminded of how her own mother, Margaret, had helped to raise the boy and his sister Christina after the deaths of both their mother and stepmother. Even then, Isaac had been a difficult youth, sullen and resentful.

Now Isaac Brant was a father himself, married to Mary Hill, with several small children. Joseph had tried to keep the young man out of trouble by giving him Native business to attend to, even employing him at times as his secretary. But the youth was jealous of his father's authority. This was clearly demonstrated by his total disregard for the information about the American peace proposal that he was supposed to deliver to the western Natives at the Maumee River.

Isaac Brant had murdered a man in cold blood sometime in 1795. The victim, a white man, had been a deserter from Anthony Wayne's army. A saddle-maker, he'd settled at the Grand River, and undoubtedly been made welcome by Joseph Brant, who wanted the settlement to be open to everyone.

Isaac was never tried for the crime, although it is well-documented. Reportedly, Joseph had hoped his son would have to answer for it, but the authorities did not pursue the matter after they decided the hapless victim was a vagabond.

The incident that ended Isaac's life happened when the local Natives went to the head of Lake Ontario to receive their annual presents. Afterward, some of them had gathered in one of the local inns for some camaraderie. There are many different versions of the story, but apparently Joseph was in one room of the two-roomed establishment and Isaac in the other.

Isaac got drunk and began calling his father names in front of the other patrons, verbally abusing him in the most foul terms and language. When Joseph entered the door of the room Isaac was in, his son slashed at him with a knife. Joseph put up a hand to defend himself and got cut. At almost the same time, Joseph hit Isaac on the head with a dirk, a small sword. Others stepped in and pulled the two apart.

All accounts agree that Joseph struck Isaac in self-defence. Isaac refused to let the head wound he'd sustained be dressed. It didn't appear too serious anyway, but two days later Isaac died, at home at the Grand River.

No one blamed Joseph but, distraught, he immediately surrendered his commission to the Indian Department. Lord Dorchester refused to accept it.

Joseph Brant took care of Isaac's family after the tragedy and later was able to get some military land for them. As Rev. John Stuart of Kingston explained it, Isaac had gotten himself in with one of the dissident groups at the Grand River that were unhappy with Joseph Brant.

There were a number of different factions in the Grand River settlement. Some were opposed to having whites as neighbours, others didn't want to give up the old ways and learn how to farm. The Canajoharie Mohawks in the settlement sometimes disagreed with the Mohawks from Fort Hunter, and vice versa, and some just plain didn't like Joseph Brant, the one man they blamed for the loss of their Mohawk Valley home.

20

The Cycle of Life

Three days before 1795 ended, Molly Brant's daughter Susanna, age twenty-three, died at Kingston. She and her husband, Ensign Henry LeMoine, had also just lost their young son, Edward William.

Less than four months later, Molly herself died, on April 16, 1796, at the Kingston home of Magdalene and John Ferguson. She was sixty, the same age Sir William had been when he died. Sources don't tell us what ended Molly's life, suggesting only that she'd been sick most of the winter. Perhaps it was the fever that Rev. John Stuart described in a letter he wrote that summer.

Many in the settlement had been sick "with an intermitting and remitting Fever," Stuart wrote. "I had a violent attack of it, in August last, and after being partly well recovered, a dangerous Relapse; But, thanks be to God, my Health is again perfectly restored — My eldest son George was confined with the same Fever for near three months. And indeed not one of our Family has not had either this Fever or the Fever and Ague during the spring season."

The Mohawk elders teach that life, like everything else, has its cycle, and Molly Brant had reached the end of hers.

Molly's longtime friend and priest, Rev. John Stuart, conducted her funeral, as he had that of Sir William Johnson twenty-two years earlier. She was buried in St. George's burying ground, which is today the site of St. Paul's Anglican Church, on the corner of Queen and Montreal Streets in Kingston. No one has yet found a trace of her grave marker. There is a possibility that it was lost during a fire at St. Paul's in 1854.

Molly didn't live to see the final family tragedy. In June, the young widower, Henry LeMoine, came to court his late wife's sister, Mary, who was two years older than Susanna. Mary seemed quite willing to accept the young man, and LeMoine went to the Ferguson home in Kingston to get Magdalene's permission to marry her sister. Magdalene, by then the oldest of Molly's family, refused. To everyone's shock and horror, LeMoine put a gun to his head and shot himself dead, right there in the Fergusons' parlour.

St. Paul's Churchyard, Kingston. Molly Brant's final resting place.

*

The same year that Molly died, her stepson Sir John Johnson, that champion of Native causes, returned to Canada. During the four years he'd been in England he had sought further compensation for the Mohawk Valley properties he'd lost during the American Revolution. He'd had little success. Shortly after his return, he was appointed to the Legislative Council of Lower Canada (Quebec), and he took back his position as head of the Indian Department.

In his private life, both before and after his absence from Canada, Sir John was almost obsessive about buying up land for himself. He owned several residences, including one in Kingston. He also had a chateau in Montreal and a house in Williamstown on the Raisin River where he had built a sawmill and a gristmill. He may never have lived in the house.

Sir John also built a house on the south shore of the St. Lawrence, opposite Montreal, on Mont Saint Grégoire. He named the house Mount Johnson after the Mohawk Valley house where he'd been born, located near Amsterdam, New York. Most of the time he lived in Montreal with his wife, Polly, and their children, who numbered between ten and fourteen.

When he had married Polly Watts in 1773, Sir John had settled his common-law wife, Clarissa, and their two children, William and Margaret (Peggy), in a comfortable house in Schenectady, New York. He continued to pay Clarissa an annuity of one thousand pounds.

In 1809, Lady Johnson (Polly) took a trip to England on her own, and while she was gone Sir John invited Clarissa to Montreal. Sources say they had a quiet reunion, and for the rest of their lives the two maintained their fondness for each other.

After Polly died in 1815, Sir John and Clarissa's daughter Peggy (born in 1765), came to live with her father at Mount Johnson, as his companion and housekeeper.

The story goes that Peggy had gotten the church warden's permission to use the Johnson family pew in the church back home, a church built by Sir William, who had said Clarissa was not good enough to bear his grandchildren.

Sir John lived to the age of eighty-eight. His 1830 funeral by all accounts was grand. Among those attending were three hundred Natives, who considered him a "friend and fellow warrior." After her father's death, Peggy went to England, where she spent her final years.

*

Joseph Brant, like other Loyalist captains at the end of the American Revolution, had been promised the usual allotment of three thousand acres, plus fifty acres each for his wife and children. Joseph had been formally commissioned by Governor Haldimand as captain in the Indian Department in 1780.

Later, Joseph bought from the Mississauga a tract of land he'd had his eye on at Burlington Bay, at the western tip of Lake Ontario. Lieutenant-Governor Simcoe, who didn't think one group of Natives should be able to buy land from another (it made it seem as if they were independent), insisted that all land sales had to be made according to British law. As a result, the Indian Department purchased the land from the king and then re-conveyed it to Joseph Brant.

Joseph fumed. If whites could buy land, why not the Natives? He had expected that the Natives' land at the Grand River would be like their land in the Mohawk Valley — theirs to do with as they wanted.

Joseph Brant wanted to develop the Grand River settlement into an important town, and he invited the whole of the Five Nations, and white Loyalists as well, to join him there. Before long the settlement even included some deserters from American general Anthony Wayne's army.

Joseph Brant let it be known that the strip of land at the Grand River that Governor Haldimand had granted to the Mohawks in 1784 was not big enough for the Natives living there to sustain themselves by hunting, and many of them were not interested in farming. If they could sell any land they didn't need, the money they'd receive would provide a living. The Six Nations people below the border were selling their lands, so why shouldn't those at the Grand River?

The Grand River Mohawks made an official request for a survey that would indicate the exact location of their grant and exactly how many acres they owned. To everyone's surprise, that survey revealed that the original grant did not go as far as the river's source, as had been written. The king hadn't owned all the land in the Haldimand Grant; part of it still belonged to the Mississauga.

The Simcoe Patent of 1793, drawn up in accordance with the new survey, still shorted the Natives by 275,000 acres. Simcoe told the Natives they couldn't sell any land to anyone except themselves or the king. When the Natives objected, Simcoe turned the matter over to Lord Dorchester.

Early in 1796, Lord Dorchester agreed to allow the Natives to sell land, provided it was first offered to the king. Joseph Brant rejected that immediately. The Natives were not subjects of the king! He decided he'd go by Haldimand's original deed, which meant the Natives would need to buy that land at the source of the river from the friendly Mississauga.

It might have happened that way too, except that Lord Dorchester had decided to give up his office and return to England. So, too, had Simcoe, who requested a leave of absence because he was unwell.

To this day there continue to be unresolved issues between the Six Nations of the Grand River and the Ontario and Canadian governments over the disposition of the land within the Haldimand Tract and the management of the money and assets received from it.

In 1789, Joseph had been able to get his Mohawks payments in goods and cash for lands they still owned at Canajoharie. The Treaty of Albany in 1797 settled all Native claims in the state of New York. It was signed by the American commissioners; Joseph Brant, representing the Grand River Natives; and John Deserontyon, agent for the Bay of Quinte Mohawks.

By this time, Joseph was ready to build on the land at Burlington Bay that he'd earlier bought from the Mississauga. There was still a lot of tension between factions at the Grand River settlement, and Joseph often found himself looking over his shoulder, thinking one of Isaac's former cohorts might be looking to finish the job Isaac had started. Even Joseph's old friends Aaron and David Hill, who had settled with him at the Grand River, had gone back to live with Deserontyon's Mohawks on the Bay of Quinte after frequent disagreements with Brant.

Joseph got along well with Molly's sons-in-law, especially Dr. Robert Kerr and Magdalene's husband, John Ferguson. He was also good friends with Brant Johnson, Molly's stepson, and Johnson's daughters, one of whom married lawyer Alexander Stewart, a man with whom Joseph often did business.

From a distance, Joseph Brant's grand house on Burlington Bay resembled Johnson Hall, the Mohawk Valley mansion of Sir

William Johnson and Molly that Joseph remembered with fondness. From behind the Burlington Bay house there was a trail back to the Grand River so that Joseph could easily travel back and forth when he wanted to visit.

*

Both of the men who had married Molly Brant's stepdaughters predeceased her. Guy Johnson, whose wife had been Sir William's daughter Mary, had always seen to it that the Native leaders were looked after lavishly, so much so that, after an inquiry into Indian Department expenses, he'd been relieved of his duties. Sir John Johnson had replaced him as Indian commissioner. Guy Johnson died in England in 1788, a pauper.

Molly's friend and supporter, Daniel Claus, who left future historians an invaluable legacy of numerous journals and letters, died in Wales in 1787. His widow, Nancy, Sir William Johnson's daughter, died around 1798. The couple's son William Claus later became Deputy Superintendent of Indian Affairs. He served as lieutenant-colonel in the 1st Lincoln Regiment and fought in the War of 1812.

Brant Johnson, Sir William's oldest son by an unknown Mohawk woman, had married a white girl at the same time as Joseph Brant married Peggie, and had served in Butler's Rangers as a scout. His wife was said to have been able to speak several languages, and their blonde-haired daughters had all gone to school in Montreal with Molly's children. The date of Brant Johnson's death is unknown.

William of Canajoharie, first reported killed at the Battle of Oriskany in 1777, was later said to have been wounded in a military incident in the early 1790s, leaving him crippled for life.

William, who it was later determined died in 1795, left at least one child, a son named Moses.

Of all Molly Brant's children, only Elizabeth, Margaret, and Anne had families that produced another generation. And although Anne, Molly's youngest, and her husband, Captain Hugh Earl, had three daughters, Ann, Mary, and Jane, none of them had any children. Anne herself died in 1818.

Margaret and George Farley had four children: Daniel, the only one to remain in Kingston, Thomas, Mary Ann, and Fanny. The others all went to live in England, where, in 1831, following the death of her husband, Margaret joined them. Before leaving Canada, Margaret took a trip to the Mohawk Valley to see Johnson Hall, the fabled family home, for the last time. Margaret died sometime between 1844 and 1846, in England.

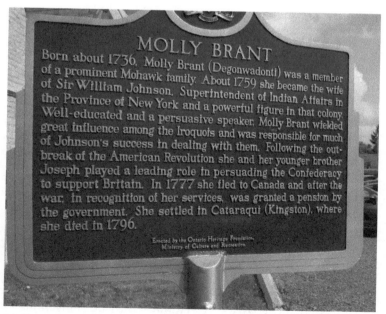

Molly Brant plaque at St. Paul's Churchyard.

Susanna had died around the same time as her only child, and Magdalene and John Ferguson's children all died very young. Molly's daughter Mary neither married nor had children.

Elizabeth and Dr. Robert Kerr had five children: William Johnson, Walter, Robert Joseph, Nancy, and Mary Margaret. Some of their descendants still live in Canada today.

William Johnson Kerr fought at Queenston Heights in the War of 1812, alongside his cousin John Brant, youngest son of Joseph. Captain Kerr led a large group of Native warriors, two hundred of whom were from Brantford, at Beaver Dams on June 24, 1813.

Eight years later, William Johnson Kerr addressed a memorial to the Duke of York, requesting a pension for himself, but also outlining the crucial part the Natives had played in the Battle of Beaver Dams. He had previously tried unsuccessfully to get official recognition for the Natives' winning the battle against the Americans. In 1828, William married his second cousin, Elizabeth Brant, youngest daughter of Joseph.

Another of Elizabeth's sons, Dr. Robert Kerr Jr., married his cousin, Mary Ann Farley, and went with her to live in England.

Molly's son George must have stayed with the family until sometime after 1792 when his name was listed among those who donated funds toward the building of the Anglican church in Cataraqui. He was twenty-four at the time. George Johnson later married a Cayuga girl and lived among her people, near Brantford, where he farmed. He is also said to have taught school for many years. A gentle man, he was well-liked and affectionately referred to as "Big" George. He died in 1826, leaving no children.

Joseph Thayendanegea Brant, Molly's beloved younger brother, died on November 24, 1807. He was sixty-four. Joseph was first buried in Burlington, but many years later, in 1850, his remains were moved to a special tomb at the side of his Mohawk

Chapel in Brantford. The remains of his son John, who died in a cholera epidemic in 1832, rest there beside him.

After Joseph's death, Catherine moved the family back to the Grand River settlement that she preferred. Catherine Brant died in 1837, exactly thirty years after Joseph.

At the end of the War of 1812, John Brant and his sister Elizabeth returned to live in their father's fine home on Burlington Bay. It was said that these two youngest children of Joseph's were the most like him in personality.

*

Around the time that Lieutenant-Governor John Graves Simcoe was preparing to go back to England for health reasons (1795), Rev. John Stuart's eldest son, George Okill Stuart, was teaching at Kingston's Grammar School. Among George's students were a number of his younger brothers and sisters.

George's own education had been interrupted because of the family's financial straits, but in 1798 he went to Harvard College. In 1801 he was ordained a priest by the Bishop of Quebec, Jacob Mountain.

In a letter dated August 29, 1811, to Bishop Mountain, Rev. George Okill Stuart reported the death of his father, John, after a week-long illness. Stuart was seventy-one.

Epilogue

There is little factual evidence about Molly Brant's early years. Fortunately, much of Sir William Johnson's business and political activities, and his work among the Mohawk, was well-documented, as was that of Joseph Brant. Because these two were significant figures in her life, we can infer parts of Molly's story from theirs.

There is nothing to indicate that Molly Brant ever visited Joseph's settlement at the Grand River, although she did return to Niagara on several occasions. She may have been aware of the animosity many of her people felt toward her brother and preferred to stay with her daughters in Kingston where the government had provided her with a comfortable home.

In February 1841, when Upper and Lower Canada became the United Province of Canada, Kingston was named its capital. The first Parliament opened there in June 1841 in a converted hospital building, pending the construction of the new Legislative Building. The glory was short-lived.

In 1844, the capital was moved to Montreal, then Toronto, followed by Quebec City, and finally Ottawa. But Kingston has the distinction of being Canada's first capital.

When Molly Brant died in 1796 she left her Kingston home to her eldest surviving daughter, Magdalene, who passed it on to her younger sister Margaret Farley. During the two years prior to Margaret's move to England there were questions about the ownership of the house, and at times Margaret was threatened with eviction.

After Margaret died in the mid-1840s, the property went to her widowed daughter-in-law Jemima Farley, the wife of Margaret's son Daniel. Jemima maintained the place until her death in 1875. By 1892 the assessment rolls indicate that neither Molly's house nor Joseph's was still standing.

As part of the Kingston Archaeological Master Plan Study, archaeological testing was conducted on the former site of Molly Brant's house in 1988, prior to the construction of the Rideaucrest Home that occupies the site today. Because of Molly Brant's historical significance to Canada, and as a result of the findings from the initial dig, salvage excavations took place on the property in 1989.

Some of the items that were unearthed, which could be attributed to Molly and her family, were small, coloured beads, such as those often used to decorate Mohawk clothing, bone hair pins and combs, ivory and bone toothbrushes, a finger ring with an amethyst stone, and glassware and crystal stemware that could indicate the owners' elevated status in society.

In 1825, construction began on a new stone church to replace the first St. George's, built in 1792. Sometime later, Molly Brant's old church was moved to another location so that a new business could be built on the site. The little church ended its days as a cabinetmaker's shop.

Photo by Mark Bergin.

Cairn and sculptured bust of Molly Brant at Rideaucrest Home, Kingston, Ontario.

The new church, a magnificent domed building at King Street East and Johnson Street in Kingston, became a cathedral in the newly established Diocese of Ontario in 1862, and George Okill Stuart, who had succeeded his father, Rev. John Stuart, as Rector of Kingston, was appointed the first dean.

Inside the Cathedral Church of St. George, on the right side wall, is a memorial to Molly Brant. Dedicated in 1984 by the United Empire Loyalists' Association of Canada, Kingston District, it reads:

> Molly Brant 1736–1797. Molly (Mary) Brant was a daughter of influential parents living in the upper Mohawk Valley of New York. Like her warrior statesman brother, Joseph, she bridged the gap between Indian and White cultures. Through her influence and contacts with the Iroquois, and her association with the British Johnson family, she helped establish and manage the important Iroquois alliance with the British during the American Revolution. She moved to Kingston after the war and she and her children by Sir William Johnson became key members of Kingston society. She was the only female founding member of St. George's.

In 1986 Canada Post issued a commemorative stamp in honour of Molly Brant. Designed by Sara Tyson, the stamp depicts Molly with three faces, indicative of the three roles she played during her lifetime: Mohawk clan mother in Iroquois society, staunch supporter of the British monarchy, and Loyalist diplomat in Canada.

The Canadian government recognized Molly Brant as a Person of National Historic Significance in 1994, the same year that the Anglican Church of Canada added the names of both Rev. John Stuart and Molly Brant to their official calendar. They declared April 16 of each year a day of special prayers in the Anglican community to commemorate Molly's life.

The City of Kingston proclaimed August 25, 1996, "Molly Brant Day." The special celebration to honour this remarkable woman two hundred years after her death was a joint initiative of the City, the Mohawks of the Bay of Quinte, Kingston's Historical Board, and the Historic Sites and Monuments Board of Canada.

The day began with a full service at St. George's Cathedral, followed by a wreath-laying and Mohawk tobacco burning at St. Paul's Churchyard. According to Mohawk tradition, as the smoke from the sacred tobacco rises it carries the prayers of the people upward to the Creator. The people say they are "putting the words through."

Local dignitaries joined First Nations chiefs and other Natives at the ceremony. Chief R. Donald Maracle of the Bay of Quinte Mohawks spoke about Molly Brant's contribution to her people and to the history of this country.

Later, a plaque was dedicated at the Rideaucrest Home and a bronze bust of Molly Brant was unveiled in the eastern court-yard. The sculptor was Kingston artist John Boxtell, who had used as a model a descendant of Joseph Brant, Rachel Claus, a young woman from the Bay of Quinte Mohawks.

Today, with her head held high, "Molly's" gaze seems to be focused far beyond the Cataraqui River, as if she might be able to see all the way home to the Mohawk Valley.

Chronology of Molly Brant (1736-96)

Molly and Her Times	*Canada and the World*
1736 Birth of Molly Brant (Gonwatsijayenni)	**1736** Birth of Patrick Henry, American Patriot and orator, famous for his "Give me liberty, or give me death!" speech
1738 William Johnson arrives in the colony of New York from Ireland to manage his uncle's Mohawk Valley lands	**1738** Fort La Reine (near Portage La Prairie, Manitoba) established by explorers La Verendrye and sons as home base for their explorations in western North America
1743 March. Birth of Joseph (Thayendanegea), brother of Molly Brant	**1743** Explorer Louis-Joseph Gaultier de la Verendrye crosses the western plains almost as far as the Rocky Mountains
1753 September 9. Marriage of Margaret, mother of Molly, to Brant (Kanagaradunka)	**1753** Founding of Lunenburg, Nova Scotia.

Molly and Her Times	*Canada and the World*
1754 Molly travels to Philadelphia with other Mohawk delegates to attend council	**1754** Start of French and Indian War for control of North America, later part of the Seven Years' War between Britain and France in Europe
1755 September 8. William Johnson wounded at the Battle of Lake George	**1755** September 8. Victory for the British and their Native allies at the Battle of Lake George
1756 William Johnson made Baronet of Great Britain	**1756** Louis-Joseph de Montcalm, leader of the French troops in North America, seizes Fort Oswego
1759 Molly Brant moves into Fort Johnson, home of Sir William Johnson September. Birth of Peter Warren, first child of Molly and Sir William	**1759** September 13. Battle of the Plains of Abraham. Quebec falls to the British. Both commanders, Wolfe and Montcalm, are killed.
1761 Birth of Elizabeth, first daughter of Molly and Sir William	**1761** September 22. Coronation of King George III of Great Britain and Queen Charlotte
1763 Birth of Magdalene, daughter of Molly and Sir William	

Molly and Her Times

Canada and the World

1763 (*cont'd*)
Johnson family moves into
Johnson Hall, a Georgian-style
mansion

1763 (*cont'd*)
October 7. George III issues
Royal Proclamation, defining
the boundary between America's
white settlements and Native
territory as a line drawn down
the centre of the Appalachian
Mountains

1765
Molly's brother Joseph Brant
marries Peggie, in a British-style
ceremony

1765
Great Britain passes the Stamp
Act, the first direct tax levied on
the American Thirteen Colonies

1767
Birth of Margaret, a third daughter for Molly and Sir William

1767
Daniel Boone from North
Carolina, in defiance of the
Proclamation of 1763, trespasses
on Native hunting grounds in
Kentucky

1768
Birth of George, second son of
Molly Brant and Sir William
Johnson

1768
November 5. Treaty of Fort
Stanwix signed, setting western
limits for white settlements at the
Ohio River

James Cook leaves Plymouth,
England, on his first voyage of
discovery

1769
Sir William is granted the patent
on Kingsland, eighty thousand
acres of land, a gift from the
Mohawks

1769
Formerly part of Nova Scotia,
St. John's Island (Prince Edward
Island) becomes a separate
British colony

Molly and Her Times	Canada and the World
1771 Birth of Mary, fourth daughter of Molly Brant and Sir William Johnson Death of Peggie, wife of Joseph Brant, from tuberculosis	**1771** Samuel Hearne explores the Coppermine River in Canada Spain cedes the Falkland Islands to Britain
1772 Birth of Susanna, fifth daughter of Molly Brant and Sir William Johnson	**1772** Committees of Correspondence are formed in the Thirteen Colonies as a means of communicating with each other and coordinating action against Britain
1773 Birth of Anne, eighth child of Molly Brant and Sir William Johnson Marriage of Sir John Johnson and Polly Watts Marriage of Joseph Brant and Susannah, half-sister of his first wife, Peggie	**1773** December 16. Boston Tea Party, a protest by the Americans against British taxation, takes place in Boston Harbor Settlers from Scotland reach Pictou, Nova Scotia, aboard the *Hector*
1774 July 11. Death of Sir William Johnson July 13. Funeral of Sir William, conducted by Rev. John Stuart. Molly Brant and her family move back to Canajoharie	**1774** British Parliament passes the Quebec Act, extending the boundaries of Quebec and helping to preserve French laws and customs in the province

Molly and Her Times

Canada and the World

1775
May 31. Many members of the
Johnson family, including Molly
Brant's son Peter, leave Mohawk
Valley

August. Molly Brant attends
council in German Flats

September 25. Peter Johnson
receives the surrender of Patriot
Ethan Allen

1777
August 5. Molly sends information to Joseph Brant at
Fort Stanwix, warning of the
approaching Patriot militia

Molly and family flee to Cayuga

Molly addresses the Native council at Onondaga

Molly Brant and family arrive at
Fort Niagara

October 21. Death of Peter
Warren Johnson, Molly's oldest
son, in battle

1775
April 19. American Revolution
begins with battles at Lexington
and Concord, Massachusetts

Quebec, Nova Scotia, and Prince
Edward Island decide against
joining the Thirteen Colonies in
the American Revolution

Americans Ethan Allan and
Benedict Arnold capture British
Fort Ticonderoga and His
Majesty's Fort at Crown Point

1777
August 6. Battle of Oriskany,
part of the Saratoga Campaign,
sees Patriot militia ambushed by
Loyalist and Native forces; both
sides claim victory

October 17. After the second
Battle of Saratoga, British
General John Burgoyne surren-
ders to American troops under
General Horatio Gates

Molly and Her Times	Canada and the World
1778	**1778**
Molly moves into her own house at Fort Niagara in the summertime	France recognizes the United States, signs Treaty of Alliance in Paris
Joseph Brant's wife, Susannah, dies of tuberculosis at Niagara	Captain James Cook is the first European to discover the Hawaiian Islands
	November 11. Massacre of civilians at Cherry Valley
1779	**1779**
July 17. Molly Brant and family move to Montreal	General John Sullivan begins campaign to destroy Native villages in New York State
September 13. Molly begins return voyage toward Niagara	August 29. Native and Loyalist forces retreat at Battle of Newtown, New York
September 29. Molly and family arrive at Carleton Island	
Joseph Brant marries Catherine Croghan	September 27. In Paris, American John Adams negotiates peace terms with Britain
	February 14. Hawaiian natives kill Captain James Cook
1780	**1780**
Molly accompanies John Butler to Montreal	In the American Revolutionary War, British troops occupy Charleston, North Carolina
Molly adopts William Lamb, a child captive	American Major-General Benedict Arnold joins the British
A house is built for Molly and family on Carleton Island	

Molly and Her Times	*Canada and the World*
	1780 (*cont'd*) Captain James Cook's ship, *Resolution*, returns to England without him
1783 Molly Brant and family leave Carleton Island	**1783** September 3. Treaty of Paris ends the American Revolutionary War
Elizabeth Johnson, Molly's eldest daughter, marries Dr. Robert Kerr	The purchase of land for the Mohawks on the Bay of Quinte is finalized
1785 Molly and family members travel to Schenectady to sign legal documents transferring her Mohawk Valley lands to the U.S. Government	**1785** Fifteen-year-old Isaac Brock joins the 8th (the King's) Regiment Colonel Josiah Harmar orders construction of a military fort at the junction of the Ohio and Muskingum Rivers
1787 Molly and daughter Elizabeth Kerr visit Montreal Birth of Elizabeth's first child, William Johnson Kerr	**1787** George Washington presides over Constitutional Convention that devises new federal govern- ment for the United States Three years of government assis- tance to Loyalists in Canada ends

Molly and Her Times	Canada and the World
1791	**1791**
At Niagara, Molly Brant attends meeting with Aupaumut, a Native on a peace mission on behalf of the Americans	Constitutional Act divides the old colony of Quebec into Upper and Lower Canada, each with its own elected assembly and appointed upper house
Molly's daughter Magdalene marries John Ferguson	
1792	**1792**
Molly and son George Johnson contribute financially to the building of St. George's Anglican Cathedral in Kingston	July 8. Lieutenant-Governor John Graves Simcoe and his executive council are sworn in at Kingston
September 17. Molly and daughters attend opening of Parliament in Newark	King Louis XVI of France is arrested in French Revolution. The monarchy is abolished and the First French Republic is established.
1793	**1793**
June 5. Molly attends wedding of daughter Susanna to Ensign Henry LeMoine, having attended the king's birthday ball in Newark the previous evening	Lieutenant-Governor Simcoe passes the Act Against Slavery, abolishing the importation of slaves into Upper Canada
	French King Louis XVI and Queen Marie Antoinette are sentenced to death and later beheaded by revolutionaries

Molly and Her Times	*Canada and the World*
1794 January. Death of Molly's daughter, Elizabeth Johnson Kerr, in childbirth Molly, then in Niagara, returns home to Kingston accompanied by Elizabeth Simcoe	**1794** November 19. Britain signs Jay's Treaty with the United States, agreeing to withdraw from forts on the American side of the border by June 1796 August 20. Western Natives routed at the Battle of Fallen Timbers
1795 Molly helps Lieutenant-Governor Simcoe to recover from his illness Death of Isaac Brant, Molly's nephew and son of Joseph Brant Death of Susanna, Molly's daughter	**1795** March 12. William Lyon Mackenzie, who will become a controversial figure in political life of Upper Canada, is born in Dundee, Scotland March 29. Twenty-four-year-old Ludwig von Beethoven debuts as pianist in Vienna, Austria
1796 April 16. Death of Molly Brant in Kingston	**1796** February 1. York (Toronto) becomes the capital of Upper Canada, replacing Newark
1807 November 24. Death of Joseph Brant, brother of Molly	**1807** June 22. British board the *USS Chesapeake*, seeking deserters, a provocation leading to the War of 1812
1818 Death of Anne, youngest daughter of Molly Brant	**1818** Forty-ninth parallel established as the border between the United States and Canada, from Lake of the Woods to the Rockies

Molly and Her Times	*Canada and the World*
1826	**1826**
Death of George Johnson, Molly's youngest son	Royal Engineer, Lieutenant-Colonel John By, designs the Rideau Canal from Kingston to the Ottawa River
1844	**1844**
Death of Margaret (Johnson) Farley, third daughter of Molly Brant	October 22. Birth of Louis Riel, leader of the Métis people and founder of Manitoba
1984	**1984**
Dedication of memorial to Molly Brant at St. George's Cathedral, Kingston, by United Empire Loyalists' Association of Canada	Marc Garneau, on U.S. shuttle *Challenger*, becomes first Canadian astronaut in space
1986	**1986**
Canada Post issues commemorative postage stamp in honour of Molly Brant	Canada forces economic sanctions against South Africa in protest of its system of apartheid
1994	**1994**
Molly Brant is declared a Person of National Historic Significance by the Canadian Government	January 1. North American Free Trade Agreement (NAFTA), the world's largest free trade region, goes into effect in Canada, the United States, and Mexico
1996	**1996**
August 25. Kingston, Ontario, declares Molly Brant Day two hundred years after her death	The Canadian Mint releases a two-dollar circulating coin, ceasing production of two-dollar notes

Selected Bibliography

Primary Sources

Anglican Diocese of Eastern Ontario Archives, Kingston, ON. *Episopal Records.* Box 1, files 2-2, 2-3, and 2-4.

Lennox and Addington County Museum and Archives, Napanee, ON. *Celia B. File Papers.* Box 5: "Letters & etc." File 26, CFC 658, "Mohawk Council." Box 6: "Bay of Quinte Mohawks." CFC 821–838, "Historical Notes." CFC 849–854, "The Six Nations." CFC 849, "Notebook of research on Mohawks; Among the Six Nations, by Mrs. Celia File."

Queen's University Archives, Kingston, ON. *Molly Brant Collection.* Location 2999. "Research notes, photocopies of articles, manuscript relating to Molly Brant (probably written by Celia B. File)."

Books

Blakeley, Phyllis R., and John N. Grant, eds. *Eleven Exiles: Accounts of Loyalists in the American Revolution*. Toronto: Dundurn, 1982.

Bolton, Jonathan, and Claire Wilson. *Joseph Brant: Mohawk Chief*. North American Indians of Achievement Series. New York: Chelsea House Publishers, 1992.

Bothwell, Robert. *A Short History of Ontario*. Edmonton, AB: Hurtig Publishers Ltd., 1986.

Boyce, Gerald E. *Historic Hastings*. Belleville, ON: Hastings County Council, 1967.

Brant, Beth, ed. *I'll Sing till the Day I Die: Conversations with Tyendinaga Elders*. Toronto: McGilligan Books, 1995.

Coffin, Howard, Will Curtis, and Jane Curtis. *Guns Over the Champlain Valley: A Guide to Historic Military Sites and Battlefields*. Woodstock, VT: The Countryman Press, 2005.

Feister, Lois M., and Bonnie Pulis. "Molly Brant: Her Domestic and Political Roles in 15th Century New York." In *Northeastern Indian Lives*, edited by Robert S. Grumet, 295–320. Amherst: University of Massachusetts Press, 1996.

Forster, Merna. "Molly Brant, Mohawk Diplomat." In *100 Canadian Heroines: Famous and Forgotten Faces*. Toronto: Dundurn, 2004.

Fryer, Mary Beacock. *King's Men: The Soldier Founders of Ontario*. Toronto: Dundurn, 1980.

Graymont, Barbara. *The Iroquois in the American Revolution*. Syracuse, NY: Syracuse University Press, 1972.

Grenville, John H., et al. *Illustrated Guide to Monuments, Memorials and Markers in the Kingston Area*. Kingston: Plaque Committee, Kingston Historical Society, 2000.

Griffis, William Elliot. *Sir John Johnson and the Six Nations*. N.p.: Dodd, Mead & Co., 1891.

Huey, Lois M., and Bonnie Pulis. *Molly Brant: A Legacy of Her Own*. Youngstown, NY: Old Fort Niagara Association Inc., 1997.

Jasonoff, Maya. *Liberty's Exiles: American Loyalists in the Revolutionary World*. New York: Alfred A. Knopf, 2011.

Johnston, Jean. *Wilderness Women: Canada's Forgotten History*. Toronto: Peter Martin Associates Ltd., 1973.

Kelsay, Isabel Thompson. *Joseph Brant 1743–1807: Man of Two Worlds*. Syracuse, NY: Syracuse University Press, 1984.

Paxton, James W. *Joseph Brant and His World: 18th Century Mohawk, Warrior and Statesman*. Toronto: James Lorimer & Co. Ltd., 2008.

Perdue, Theda, ed. *Sifters: Native American Women's Lives*. New York: Oxford University Press, 2001.

Porter, Tom. *And Grandma Said ... Iroquois Teachings As Passed Down Through the Oral Tradition*. USA: Xlibris Corp., 2008.

Preston, Richard A., ed. *Kingston Before the War of 1812: A Collection of Documents*. Toronto: The Champlain Society for the Government of Canada. University of Toronto Press, 1959.

Randle, Martha Champion. "Iroquois Women: Then and Now." In *Iroquois Women: An Anthology*, edited by W.G. Spittal, 136–48. Ohsweken, ON: Iroquois Reprints, 1990.

Robinson, Helen Caister. *Mistress Molly, the Brown Lady: Portrait of Molly Brant*. Toronto: Dundurn, 1980.

Shafer, Ann Eastlack. "The Status of Iroquois Women." In *Iroquois Women: An Anthology*, edited by W.G. Spitall, 71–135. Ohsweken, ON: Iroquois Reprints, 1990.

Snow, Dean R. "Theyanoguin." In *Northeastern Indian Lives*, edited by Robert S. Grumet, 208–26. Amherst: University of Massachusetts Press, 1996.

Thomas, Earle. *The Three Faces of Molly Brant*. Kingston: Quarry Press, 1996.

Tooker, Elisabeth. "Women in Iroquois Society." In *Iroquois Women: An Anthology*, edited by W.G. Spittal, 199–216. Ohsweken, ON: Iroquois Reprints, 1990.

Young, A.H. *The Revd John Stuart D.D., U.E.L., of Kingston, U.C. and His Family: A Genealogical Study*. Kingston: Whig Press, n.d.

Journals

Bazely, Susan M. "Molly Brant: Konwatsi'tsiaienne: Who Was She Really?" *Historic Kingston* 45 (1997): 9–21.

Green, Gretchen. "Molly Brant, Catherine Brant and Their Daughters: A Study in Colonial Acculturation." *Ontario History* 71, no. 3 (September 1989).

Gross, Judith. "Molly Brant: textural representations of cultural midwifery." *American Studies* 40, no.1 (Spring 1999): 23–40.

Gundy, H. Pearson. "Molly Brant, Loyalist." *Ontario History* 45, no. 3 (Summer 1953) 97–108.

Johnston, Jean. "Ancestry and Descendants of Molly Brant." *Ontario History* 63, no. 2 (June 1971) 87–92.

Thomas, Earle. "Molly Brant, Mohawk Loyalist." *Kingston Historical Society*, n.d.

Newspapers

Lukits, Ann. "Molly Brant: Matron of the Mohawks." *The Kingston Whig Standard*, July 1, 2006.

Pamphlets, Bulletins

Herrington, M. Eleanor. "Captain John Deserontyou and the Mohawk Settlement at Deseronto." *Bulletin of the*

Departments of History and Political and Economic Science in Queen's University, Kingston, Ontario, Canada, no. 41 (November 1921).

"Old St. George's: Being the Story of a Church and Its Ministers in a Historic Centre of Upper Canada." Kingston: Uglow, 1913.

Electronic Documents

Bazely, Susan M. "Who Was Molly Brant?" *The Cataraqui Archaelogical Research Foundation*. Accessed April 14, 2011. www.carf.info/kingston-past/molly-brant.

"Early Recognized Treaties with American Indian Nations: Proceedings of Sir William with the Indians at Fort Stanwix to Settle a Boundary Line." *Center for Digital Research, University of Nebraska-Lincoln*. Accessed November 21, 2013. http://earlytreaties.unl.edu/treaty.00007.html.

"Fort Hunter." *Rootsweb*. Accessed February 1, 2014. www.rootsweb.ancestry.com/~nytryon/forthunter.html.

"The Four Kings of Canada." *Internet Archive Digital Library*. Accessed June 2, 2013. https://archive.org/details/fourkingsofcanad00lond.

Gable, Walter. "Sullivan Campaign of 1779." Accessed September, 20, 2013. www.co.seneca.ny.us/wp-content/uploads/2014/11/Chap-4-Sullivan-Campaign-of-1779.pdf.

Graymont, Barbara. "Konwatsia'tsianni (Molly Brant)." *Dictionary of Canadian Biography Online*. Accessed February 20, 2014. www.biographi.ca/en/bio/konwatsitsiaienni_4E.html.

Graymont, Barbara. "Thayendanegea." *Dictionary of Canadian Biography Online*. Accessed September, 20, 2013. www.biographi.ca/en/bio/thayendanegea_5E.html.

Johnston, C.M. "Deserontyon, John." *Dictionary of Canadian Biography Online.* Accessed September 20, 2013. www.biographi.ca/en/bio/deserontyon_john_5E.html.

Leighton, Douglas. "Claus, Christian Daniel." *Dictionary of Canadian Biography Online.* Accessed June 2, 2013. www.biographi.ca/en/bio/claus_christian_daniel_4E.html.

Morgan, Lewis. "League of the Ho-dé-no-sau-nee or Iroquois." *Internet Archive Digital Library.* Accessed February 1, 2014. https://archive.org/details/hodenosaunee00morgrich.

"Quebec Act." *Encyclopedia Britannica Online.* Accessed September 20, 2013. www.britannica.com/EBchecked/topic/486697/Quebec-Act.

"Six Nations of the Grand River." Accessed January, 25, 2015. www.ontario.ca/government/six-nations-grand-river.

Thomas, Earle. "Johnson, Sir John." *Dictionary of Canadian Biography Online.* Accessed January 14, 2014. www.biographi.ca/en/bio/johnson_john_6E.html.

Turner, Larry. "Grass, Michael." *Dictionary of Canadian Biography Online.* Accessed January 14, 2014. www.biographi.ca/en/bio/grass_michael_5E.html.

Venebles, Robert W. "An Analysis of the 1613 Tawagonshi Treaty: History of the Relations with Our Brothers." *Onondaga Nation-People of the Hills.* Accessed October 15, 2013. www.onondaganation.org/history/2012/an-analysis-of-the-1613-tawagonshi-treaty.

Index